AF594592

PEN DRAWING

An Illustrated Treatise

PEN DRAWING

An Illustrated Treatise

CHARLES D. MAGINNIS

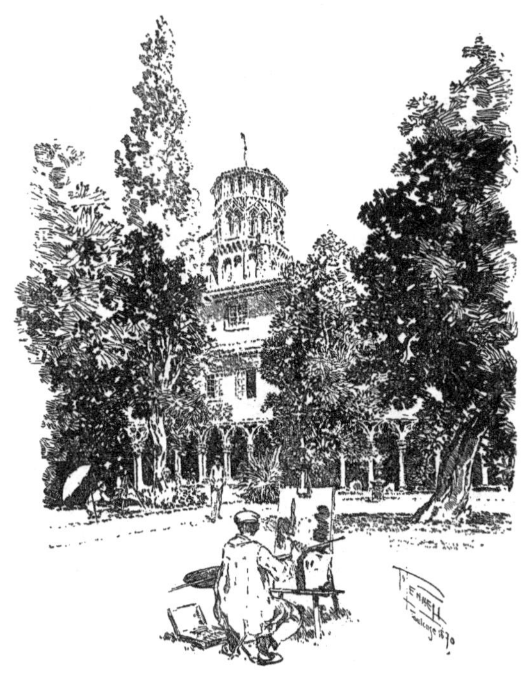

Dover Publications, Inc., Mineola, New York

Bibliographical Note

This Dover edition, first published in 2016, is an unabridged republication of the sixth edition, originally published by Bates & Guild Company, Boston, and B. T. Batsford, London, in 1913.

Library of Congress Cataloging-in-Publication Data

Names: Maginnis, Charles Donagh, 1867–1955, author.
Title: Pen drawing : an illustrated treatise / Charles Maginnis.
Description: Mineola, New York : Dover Publications, Inc., 2016. | "This Dover edition of Pen Drawing: An Illustrated Treatise, first published in 2016, is an unabridged republication of the sixth edition, originally published by Bates & Guild Company, Boston, and B.T. Batsford, London, in 1913."
Identifiers: LCCN 2016013923| ISBN 9780486810751 | ISBN 0486810755
Subjects: LCSH: Pen drawing.
Classification: LCC NC905 .M25 2016 | DDC 741.2—dc23
LC record available at http://lccn.loc.gov/2016013923

Manufactured in the United States by LSC Communications
81075502 2017
www.doverpublications.com

ACKNOWLEDGMENT

To Mr. David A. Gregg and to Mr. Bertram G. Goodhue, who have generously made special drawings for this little book, and to the Publishers who have courteously allowed me to make use of illustrations owned by them, my thanks and my cordial acknowledgments are due. C. D. M.

LIST OF ILLUSTRATIONS

CONTENTS

PEN DRAWING

An Illustrated Treatise

CHAPTER I

STYLE IN PEN DRAWING

Art, with its finite means, cannot hope to record the infinite variety and complexity of Nature, and so contents itself with a partial statement, addressing this to the imagination for the full and perfect meaning. This inadequation, and the artificial adjustments which it involves, are tolerated by right of what is known as artistic convention; and as each art has its own particular limitations, so each has its own particular conventions. Sculpture reproduces the forms of Nature, but discards the color without any shock to our ideas of verity; Painting gives us the color, but not the third dimension, and we are satisfied; and Architecture is *purely* conventional, since it does not even aim at the imitation of natural form.

The Conventions of Line Drawing

Of the kindred arts which group themselves under the head of Painting, none is based on such broad conventions as that with which we are immediately concerned — the art of Pen Drawing. In this medium, Nature's variety of color, when not positively ignored, is suggested by means of sharp black lines, of varying thickness, placed more or less closely together upon white paper; while natural form depends primarily for its representation upon arbitrary boundary lines. There is, of course, no authority in Nature for a positive outline: we see objects only by the difference in color of the other objects behind and around them. The technical capacity of the pen and ink medium, however, does not provide a value corresponding to every natural one, so that a broad interpretation has to be adopted which eliminates the less positive values; and, that form may not likewise be sacrificed, the outline becomes necessary, that light objects may stand relieved against light. This outline is the most characteristic, as it is the most indispensable, of the conventions of line drawing. To seek to abolish it only involves a resort to expedients no less artificial, and the results of all such attempts, dependent as they necessarily are upon elaboration of color, and a general indirectness of method, lack some of the best characteristics of pen drawing. More frequently, however, an elaborate color-scheme is merely a straining at the technical limitations of the pen in an effort to render the greatest possible number of values.

It may be worth while to inquire whether excellence in pen drawing consists in thus dispensing with its recognized conventions, or in otherwise taxing the technical resources of the instrument. This involves the question of

Style, — of what characteristic pen methods are, — a question which we will briefly consider.

What Constitutes "Style"

It is a recognized principle that every medium of art expression should be treated with due regard to its nature and properties. The sculptor varies his technique according as he works in wood, granite, or marble; the painter handles his water-color in quite another manner than that he would employ on an oil-painting of the same subject; and the architect, with the subtle sense of the craftsman, carries this principle to such a fine issue as to impart an individual expression even to particular woods. He knows that what may be an admirable design when executed in brass may be a very bad one in wrought-iron and is sure to be an absurdity in wood. An artistic motive for a silver flagon, too, is likely to prove ugly for pottery or cut-glass, and so on. There is a genius, born of its particular properties, in every medium, which demands individual expression. Observe, therefore, that Art is not satisfied with mere unrelated beauty of form or color. It requires that the result confess some sensible relation to the means by which it has been obtained; and in proportion as it does this, it may claim to possess that individual and distinctive charm which we call "Style." It may be said, therefore, that the technical limitations of particular mediums impose what might properly be called natural conventions; and while misguided ambition may set these conventions aside to hammer out effects from an unwilling medium, the triumph is only mechanical; Art does not lie that way.

The Province of the Pen

Ought the pen, then, to be persuaded into the province of the brush? Since the natures of the two means differ, it does not stultify the water-color that it cannot run the deep gamut of oil. Even if the church-organ be the grandest and most comprehensive of musical instruments we may still be permitted to cherish our piano. Each has its own sphere, its own reason for being. So of the pen, — the piccolo flute of the artistic orchestra. Let it pipe its high treble as merrily as it may, but do not coerce it into mimicking the bassoon.

Pen drawing is most apt to lose its individuality when it begins to assume the characteristics of wash-drawing, such as an elaborate massing of grays, small light areas, and a general indirectness of method. A painter once told me that he was almost afraid to handle the pen, — "It is so fearfully direct," he said. He understood the instrument, certainly, for if there is one characteristic more than another which should distinguish pen methods it is Directness. The nature of the pen seems to mark as its peculiar function that of picking out the really vital features of a subject. Pen drawing has been aptly termed the "shorthand

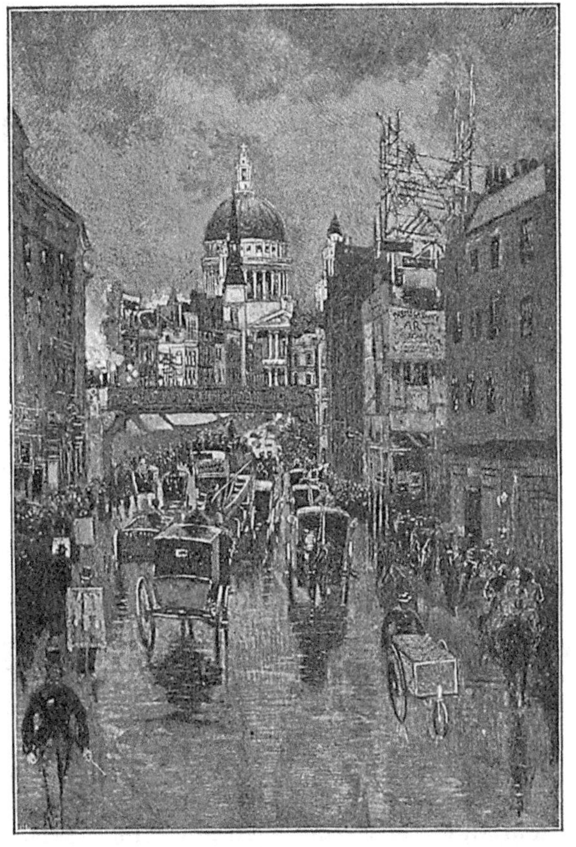

FIG. I JOSEPH PENNELL

of Art;" the genius of the pen-point is essentially epitome.

If we turn to the brush, we find its capacity such that a high light may be brought down to a minute fraction of an inch with a few swift strokes of it; whereas the tedious labor, not to speak of the actual technical difficulties, encountered in attempting such an effect of color with pen and ink, indicates that we are forcing the medium. Moreover, it is technically impossible to reproduce with the pen the low values which may be obtained with the brush; and it is unwise to attempt it. The way, for example, in which Mr. Joseph Pennell handles his pen as compared with that in which he handles his brush is most instructive as illustrating what I have been maintaining. His pen drawings are pitched in a high key,—brilliant blacks and large light areas, with often just enough half-tone to soften the effect. His wash-drawings, on the contrary, are so utterly different in manner as to have nothing in common with the others, distinguished as they are by masses of low tone and small light areas. Compare Figs. 1 and 5. Observe that there is no straining at the technical capacity of the pen or of the brush; no attempt to obtain an effect in one medium which seems to be more naturally adapted to the other. Individuality is imparted to each by a frank concession to its peculiar genius.

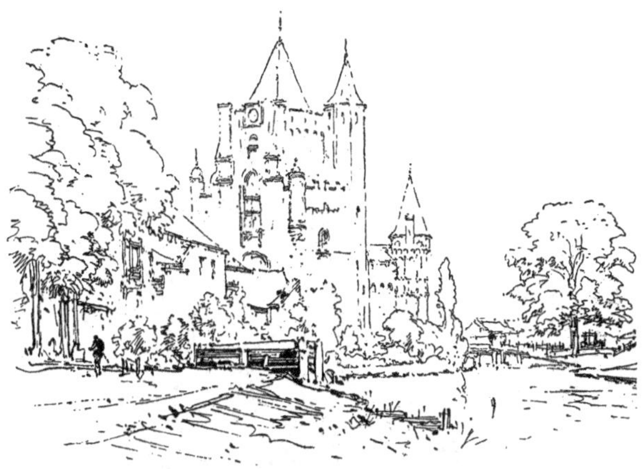

FIG. 2 MAXIME LALANNE

Examples of Good Style

I have said that the chief characteristic of pen methods is Directness. I think I may now say that the chief element of style is Economy of Means. The drawing by M. Maxime Lalanne shown in Fig. 2 is an excellent example of this economy carried to its extreme. Not a stroke could be spared, so direct and simple is it, and yet it is so complete and homogenous that nothing could be added to make it more so. The architecture is left without color, and yet we are made to feel that it is not white—this subtle suggestion of low color being obtained by a careful avoidance of any strong black notes in the rendering, which would have intensified the whites and lighted up the picture. Fig. 3, by the same artist, is even more

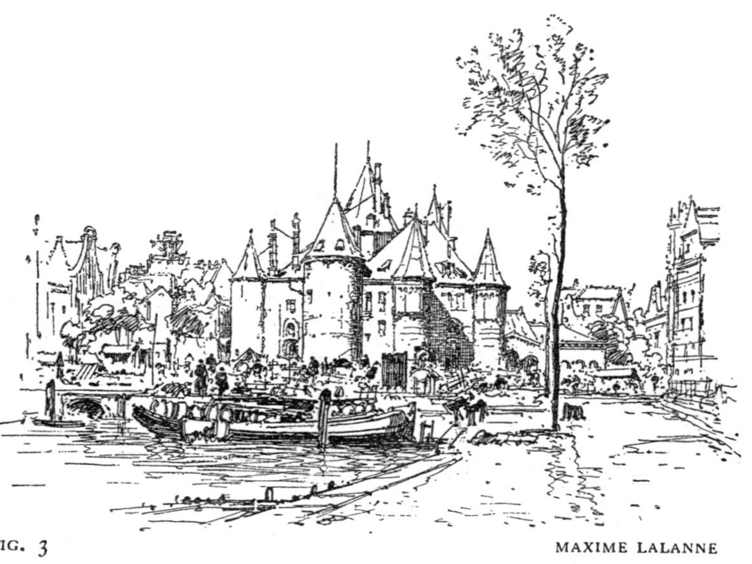

FIG. 3 MAXIME LALANNE

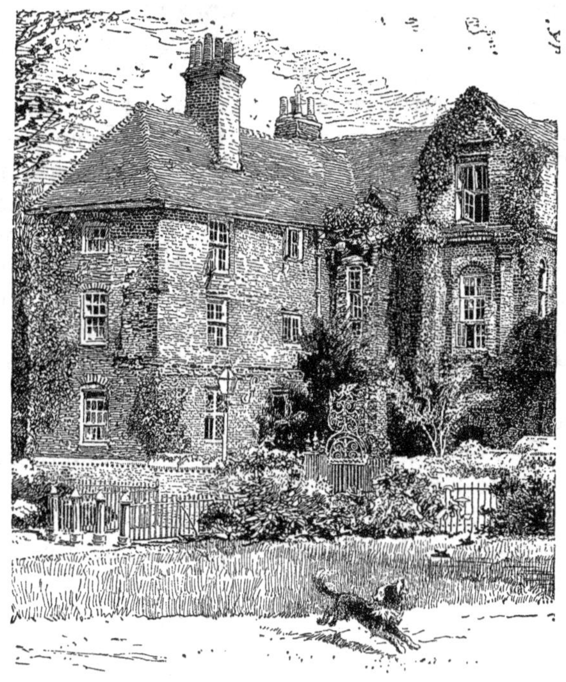

FIG. 4 FROM A PHOTOGRAPH

notable by reason of the masterly breadth which characterizes the treatment of a most complicated subject. A comparison of these with a drawing of the Restoration House, at Rochester, England, Fig. 4, is instructive. In the latter the method is almost painfully elaborate; nothing of the effect is obtained by suggestion. The technique is varied and interesting, but the whole drawing lacks that individual something which we call Style. In the Lalanne drawings we see foliage convincingly represented by means of the mere outlines and a few subtle strokes of the pen. There is no attempt at the literal rendering of natural objects in detail, all is accomplished by suggestion: and while I do not wish to be understood as insisting upon such a severely simple style, much less upon the purist theory that the function of the pen is concerned with form alone, I would impress upon the student that Lalanne's is incomparably the finer manner of the two.

Between these two extremes of method there is a wide latitude for individual choice. Contrast with the foregoing the accompanying pen drawing by Mr. Pennell, Fig. 5, which gives a

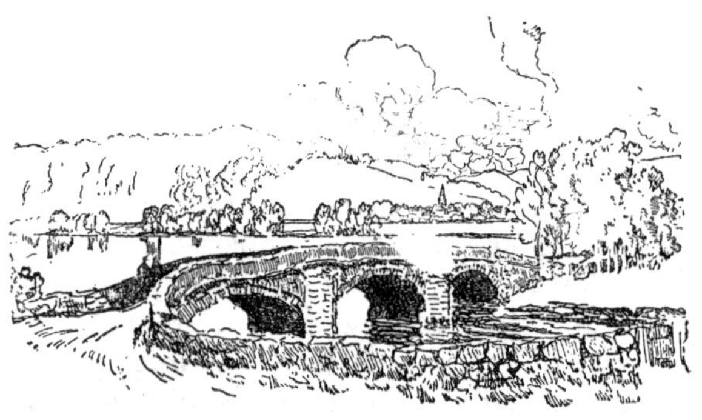

FIG. 5 JOSEPH PENNELL

A Word of Advice

fair idea of the manner of this admirable stylist. Compared with the sketches by Lalanne it has more richness of color, but there is the same fine restraint, the same nice regard for the instrument. The student will find it most profitable to study the work of this masterly penman. By way of warning, however, let me remind him here, that in studying the work of any accomplished draughtsman he is selecting a style for the study of principles, not that he may learn to mimic somebody, however excellent the somebody may be; that he must, therefore, do a little thinking himself; that he has an individuality of his own which he does not confess if his work looks like some one's else; and, finally, that he has no more right to consciously appropriate the peculiarities of another's style than he has to appropriate his more tangible property, and no more reason to do so than he has to walk or talk like him.

CHAPTER II

MATERIALS

Every illustrator has his special predilections in the matter of materials, just as he has in the matter of methods. The purpose of this chapter is, therefore, rather to assist the choice of the student by limiting it than to choose for him. It would be advisable for him to become acquainted with the various materials that I may have occasion to mention (all of them are more or less employed by the prominent penmen), and a partiality for particular ones will soon develop itself. He is reminded, however, that it is easily possible to exaggerate the intrinsic values of pens and papers; in fact the beginner invariably expects too much from them. Of course, he should not use any but the best,—even Vierge could not make a good drawing with a bad pen,—but the artistic virtues of a particular instrument are not likely to disclose themselves in the rude scratchings of the beginner. He has to master it, to "break it in," ere he can discover of what excellent service it is capable.

The student will find that most of the steel pens made for artists have but a short period

Pens

of usefulness. When new they are even more unresponsive than when they are old. At first they are disposed to give a hard, wiry line, then they grow sympathetic, and, finally, lose their temper, when they must be immediately thrown away. As a general rule, the more delicate points are better suited to the smooth surfaces, where they are not likely to get tripped up and "shaken" by the roughness in the paper.

To begin with the smaller points, the "Gillott Crow-quill" is an excellent instrument. The normal thickness of its line is extremely small, but so beautifully is the nib made that it will respond vigorously to a big sweeping stroke. I say a "sweeping stroke," as its capacity is not to be taxed for uniformly big lines. An equally delicate point, which surpasses the crow-quill in range, is "Gillott's Mapping-pen." It is astonishing how large a line may be made with this instrument. It responds most nimbly to the demands made upon it, and in some respects reminds one of a brush. It has a short life, but it may be a merry one. Mr. Pennell makes mention of a pen, "Perry's Auto-Stylo," which seems to possess an even more wonderful capacity, but of this I cannot speak from experience. A coarser, but still a small point, is the "Gillott 192"—a good pen with a fairly large range; and, for any others than the smooth papers, a pen smaller than this will probably be found undesirable for general use. A shade bigger than this is the "Gillott 303," a very good average size. Neither of these two possesses the sensitiveness of those previously mentioned, but for work demanding more or less uniformity of line they will be found more satisfactory. The smaller points are liable to lead one into the quagmire of finicalness. When we get beyond the next in size, the "Gillott 404," there is nothing about the coarse steel points to especially commend them for artistic use. They are usually stupid, unreliable affairs, whose really valuable existence is about fifteen working minutes. For decorative drawing the ordinary commercial "stub" will be found a very satisfactory instrument. Of course one may use several sizes of pens in the same drawing, and it is often necessary to do so.

Before leaving the steel pens, the "double-line pen" may be mentioned, though it has only a limited sphere. It is a two-pointed arrangement, practically two pens in one, by means of which parallel lines may be made with one stroke. Rather interesting effects can be obtained with it, but on the whole it is most valuable as a curiosity. Though somewhat out of fashion for general use, the quill of our fathers is favored by many illustrators. It is splendidly adapted for broad, vigorous rendering of foreground effects, and is almost dangerously easy to handle. Reed pens, which have somewhat similar virtues, are now little employed, and cannot be bought. They have to be cut from the natural reed, and used while fresh. For many uses in decorative drawing one of the most satisfactory instruments is the glass pen, which gives an absolutely uniform line. The point being really the end of a thin tube, the stroke may be made in any direction, a most unique characteristic in a pen. It has, however, the disadvantages of being friable and expensive; and, as it needs to be kept clean, the patent water-proof ink should not be used with it unless absolutely necessary. A flat piece of cork or rubber should be placed inside the ink-bottle when this pen is used, otherwise it is liable to be smashed by striking the bottom of the bottle. The faculty possessed by the Japanese brush of retaining its point renders it also available for use as a pen, and it is often so employed.

Inks

In drawing for reproduction, the best ink is that which is blackest and least shiny. Until a few years ago it was the custom of penmen to grind their India ink themselves; but, besides the difficulty of always ensuring the proper consistency, it was a cumbersome method, and is now little resorted to, especially as numerous excellent prepared inks are ready to hand. The better known of these prepared inks are, "Higgins' American" (general and waterproof),

Bourgeois' "Encre de Chine Liquide," "Carter's," "Winsor & Newton's," and "Rowney's." Higgins' and Carter's have the extrinsic advantages of being put up in bottles which do not tip over on the slightest provocation, and of being furnished with stoppers which can be handled without smearing the fingers. Otherwise, they cannot be said to possess superiority over the others, certainly not over the "Encre de Chine Liquide." Should the student have occasion to draw over salt-prints he will find it wise to use waterproof ink, as the bleaching acid which is used to fade the photographic image may otherwise cause the ink to run.

Papers Bristol-board is probably the most popular of all surfaces for pen drawing. It is certainly that most approved by the process engraver, whose point of view in such a matter, though a purely mechanical one, is worthy of consideration. It has a perfectly smooth surface, somewhat difficult to erase from with rubber, and which had better be scratched with a knife when any considerable erasure is necessary. As the cheap boards are merely a padding veneered on either side with a thin coating of smooth paper, little scraping is required to develop a fuzzy surface upon which it is impossible to work. Only the best board, such as Reynolds', therefore, should be used. Bristol-board can be procured in sheets of various thicknesses as well as in blocks.

Whatman's "hot-pressed" paper affords another excellent surface and possesses some advantages over the Bristol-board. It comes in sheets of various sizes, which may be either tacked down on a board or else "stretched." Tacking will be satisfactory enough if the drawing is small and is to be completed in a few hours; otherwise the paper is sure to "hump up," especially if the weather be damp. The process of stretching is as follows: Fold up the edges of the sheet all around, forming a margin about an inch wide. After moistening the paper thoroughly with a damp sponge, cover the under side of this turned-up margin with photographic paste or strong mucilage. During this operation the sheet will have softened and "humped up," and will admit of stretching. Now turn down the adhesive margin and press it firmly with the fingers, stretching the paper gently at the same time. As this essential part of the process must be performed quickly, an assistant is requisite when the sheet is large. Care should be taken that the paper is not strained too much, as it is then likely to burst when it again contracts.

Although generally employed for water-color drawing, Whatman's "cold-pressed" paper has some advantages as a pen surface. Slightly roughish in texture, it gives an interesting broken line, which is at times desirable.

A peculiar paper which has considerable

vogue, especially in France and England, is what is known as "clay-board." Its surface is composed of China clay, grained in various ways, the top of the grain being marked with fine black lines which give a gray tone to the paper, darker or lighter according to the character of the pattern. This tone provides the middle-tint for the drawing. By lightly scraping with a sharp penknife or scratcher, before or after the pen work is done, a more delicate gray tone may be obtained, while vigorous scraping will produce an absolute white. With the pen work added, it will be seen that a good many values are possible; and, if the drawing be not reduced more than one-third, it will print excellently. The grain, running as it does in straight lines, offers a good deal of obstruction to the pen, however, so that a really good line is impossible.

Thin letter-paper is sometimes recommended for pen and ink work, chiefly on account of its transparency, which obviates the necessity of re-drawing after a preliminary sketch has been worked up in pencil. Over the pencil study a sheet of the letter-paper is placed on which the final drawing may be made with much deliberation. Bond paper, however, possesses the similar advantage of transparency besides affording a better texture for the pen.

CHAPTER III

TECHNIQUE

The Individual Line

The first requirement of a good pen technique is a good Individual Line, a line of feeling and quality. It is usually a surprise to the beginner to be made aware that the individual line is a thing of consequence,—a surprise due, without doubt, to the apparently careless methods of some successful illustrators. It is to be borne in mind, however, that some illustrators are successful in spite of their technique rather than because of it; and also that the apparently free and easy manner of some admirable technicians is in reality very much studied, very deliberate, and not at all to be confounded with the unsophisticated scribbling of the beginner. The student is apt to find it just about as easy to draw like Mr. Pennell as to write like Mr. Kipling. The best way to acquire such a superb freedom is to be very, very careful and painstaking. To appreciate how beautiful the individual line may be one has but to observe the rich, decorative stroke of Howard Pyle, Fig. 66, or that of Mucha, Fig. 65, the tender outline of Boutet de Monvel, the tell-

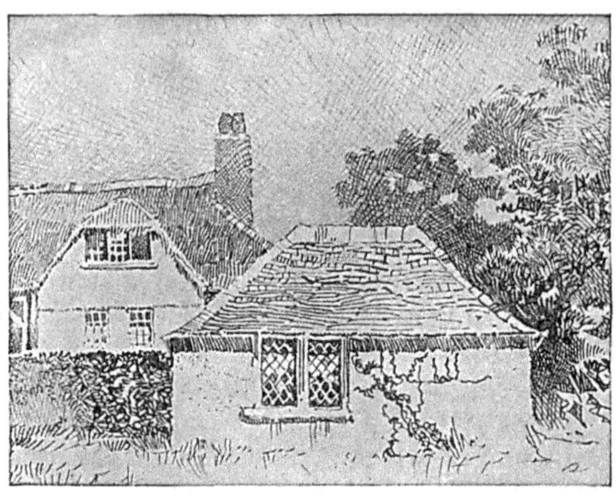

FIG. 6 B. G. GOODHUE

Copyright 1899 by the Life Publishing Company

ing, masterly sweep of Gibson, or the short, crisp line of Vierge or Rico. Compared with any of these the line of the beginner will be either feeble and tentative, or harsh, wiry, and coarse.

Variety of Line

The second requisite is Variety of Line,—not merely variety of size and direction, but, since each line ought to exhibit a feeling for the particular texture which it is contributing to express, variety of character. Mr. Gibson's manner of placing very delicate gray lines against a series of heavy black strokes exemplifies some of the possibilities of such variety. Observe, in Fig. 6, what significance is imparted to the heavy lines on the roof of

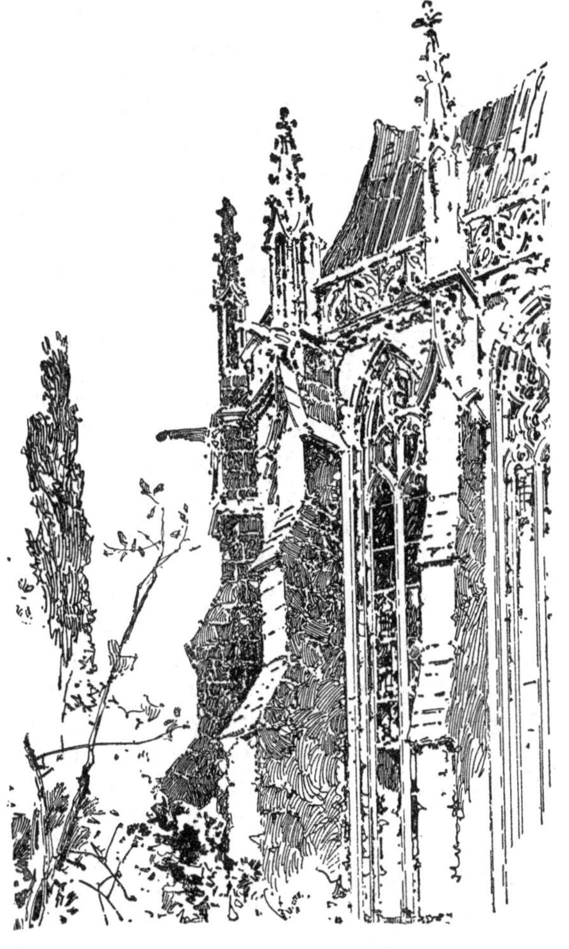

FIG. 7 HERBERT RAILTON

the little foreground building by the foil of delicate gray lines in the sky and surrounding roofs. This conjunction was employed early by Mr. Herbert Railton, who has made a beautiful use of it in his quaint architectural subjects. Mr. Railton's technique is remarkable also for the varied direction of line and its expression of texture. Note this characteristic in his drawing of buttresses, Fig. 7.

Economy of Method

The third element of good technique is Economy and Directness of Method. A tone should not be built up of a lot of meaningless strokes. Each line ought, sensibly and directly, to contribute to the ultimate result. The old mechanical process of constructing tones by cross-hatching is now almost obsolete. It is still employed by modern pen draughtsmen, but it is only one of many resources, and is used with nice discrimination. At times a cross-hatch is very desirable and very effective,—as, for example, in affording a subdued background for figures having small, high lights. A very pretty use of it is seen in the tower of Mr. Goodhue's drawing, Fig. 8. Observe here how the intimate treatment of the roofs is enhanced and relieved by the foil of closely-knit hatch on the tower-wall, and how effective is the little area of it at the base of the spire. The cross-hatch also affords a satisfactory method of obtaining deep, quiet shadows. See the archway "B" in Fig. 9.

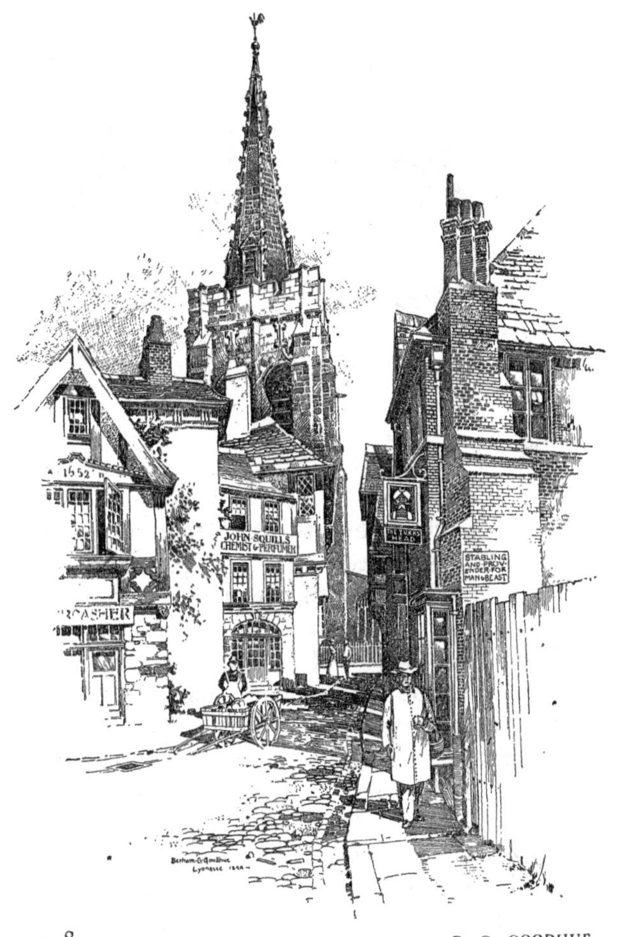

FIG. 8 B. G. GOODHUE

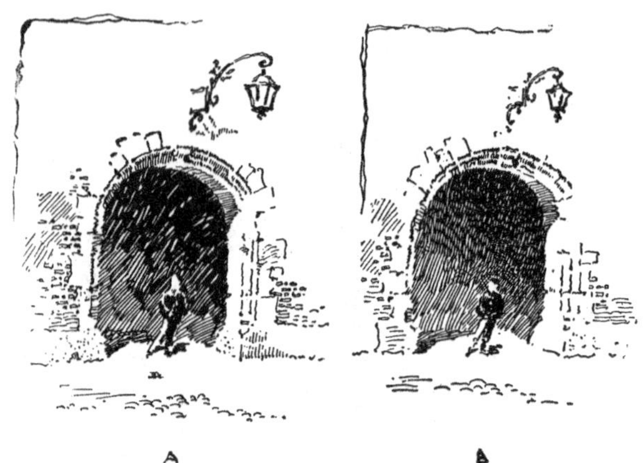

FIG. 9 C. D. M.

On the whole, however, the student is advised to accustom himself to a very sparing use of this expedient. Compare the two effects in Fig. 9. Some examples of good and bad cross-hatching are illustrated in Fig. 10. Those marked "I" and "J" may be set down as bad, being too coarse. The only satisfactory cross-hatch at a large scale would seem to be that shown in "N," where lines cross at a sharp angle; and this variety is effectively employed by figure illustrators. Perhaps no better argument against the necessity for thus building up tones could be adduced than the little drawing by Martin Rico, shown in Fig. 11. Notice what a beautiful texture he gives to the shadow where

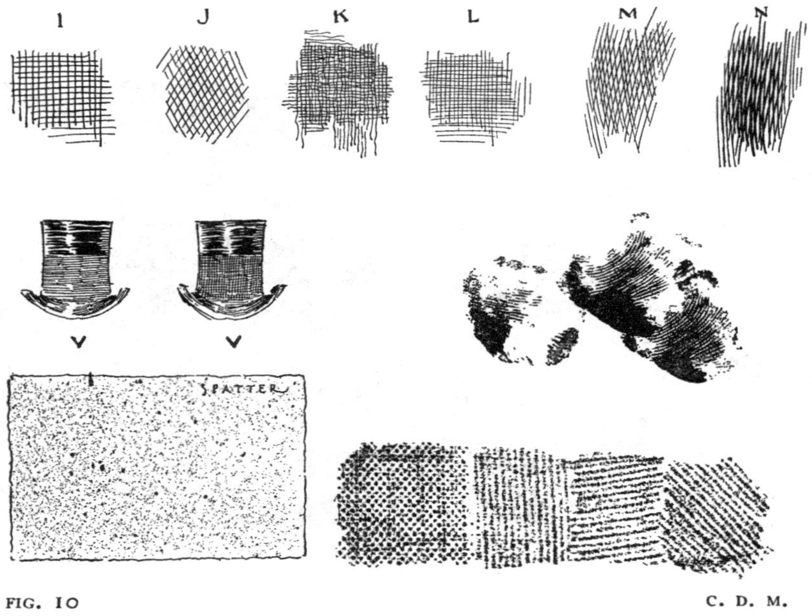

FIG. 10

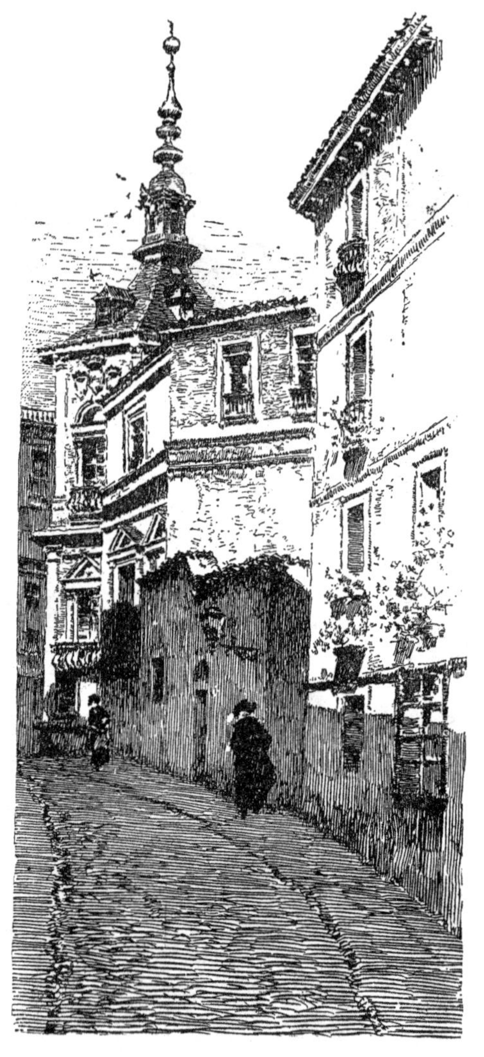

FIG. 11 MARTIN RICO

it falls on the street, how it differs from that on the walls, how deep and closely knit it all is, and yet that there is absolutely no cross-hatching. Remark, also, how the textures of the walls and roof and sky are obtained. The student would do well to copy such a drawing as this, or a portion of it, at least, on a larger scale, as much can be learned from it.

Methods of Tone-Making

I have shown various methods of making a tone in Fig. 12. It will be observed that Rico's shadow, in Fig. 11, is made up of a combination of "B" and "C," except that he uses "B" horizontally, and makes the line heavy and dragging. The clear, crisp shadows of Vierge are also worthy of study for the simplicity of method. This is beautifully illustrated in the detail, Fig. 13. It would be impossible to suggest atmosphere more vibrating with sunlight; a result due to the transparency of the shadows, the lines of which are sharp and clean, with never a suggestion of cross-hatch. Notice how the lines of the architectural shadows are stopped abruptly at times, giving an emphasis which adds to the brilliancy of the effect. The drawing of the buildings on the canal, by Martin Rico, Fig. 14, ought also to be carefully studied in this connection. Observe how the shadow-lines in this drawing, as in that previously mentioned, are made to suggest the direction of the sunlight, which is high in the heavens.

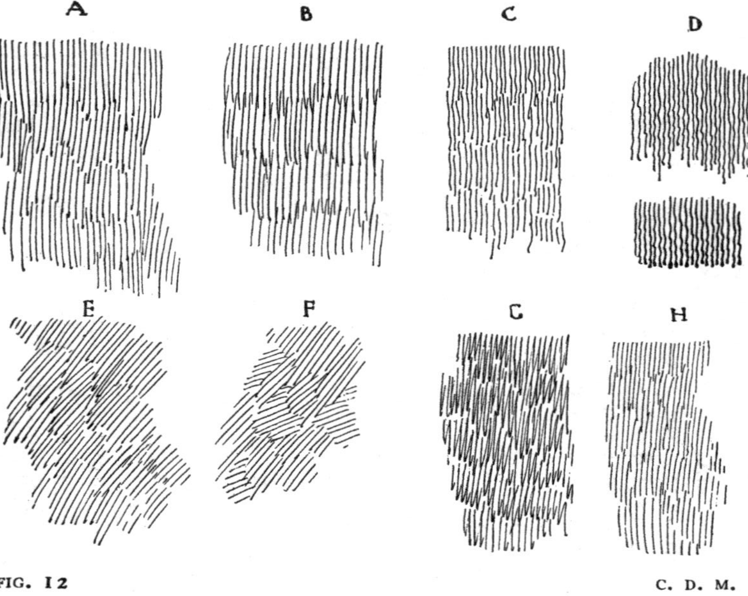

FIG. 12

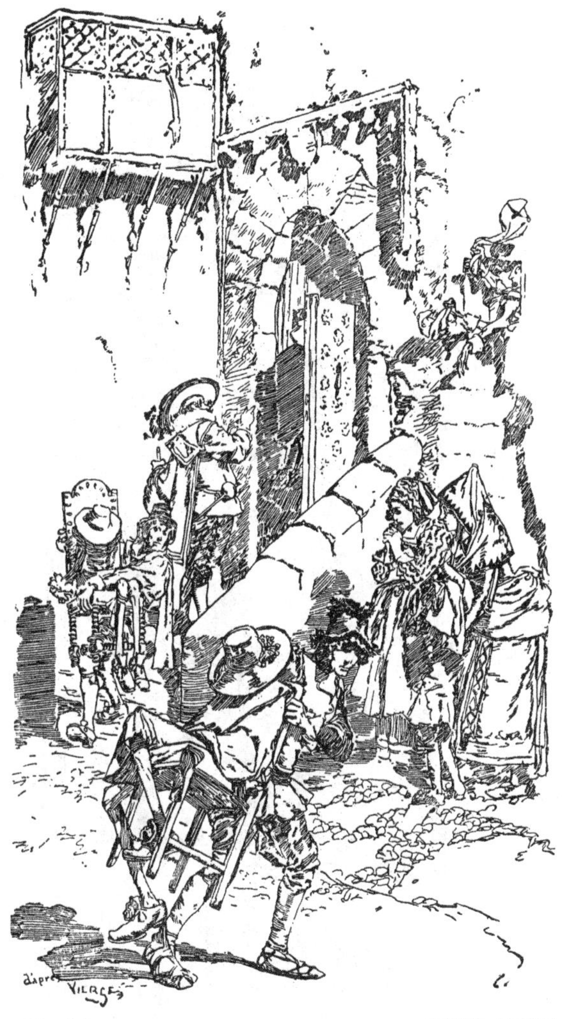

FIG. 13 DANIEL VIERGE

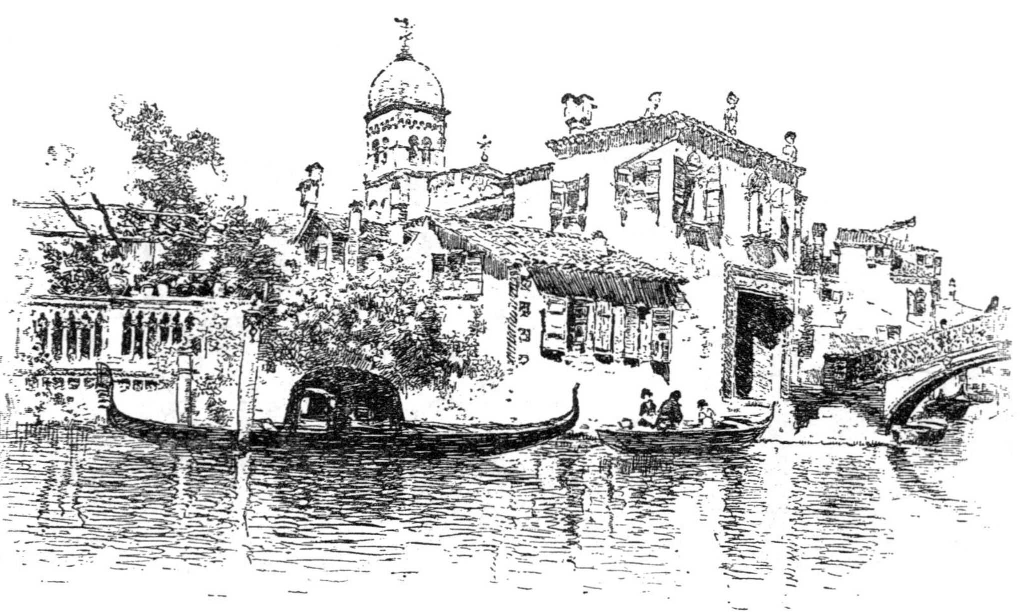

FIG. 14 MARTIN RICO

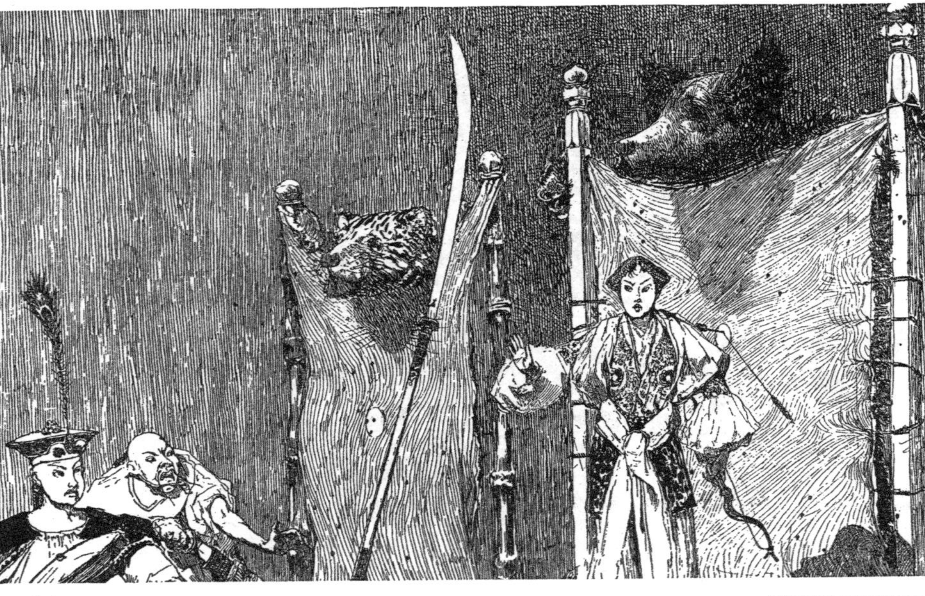

FIG. 15 ALFRED BRENNAN

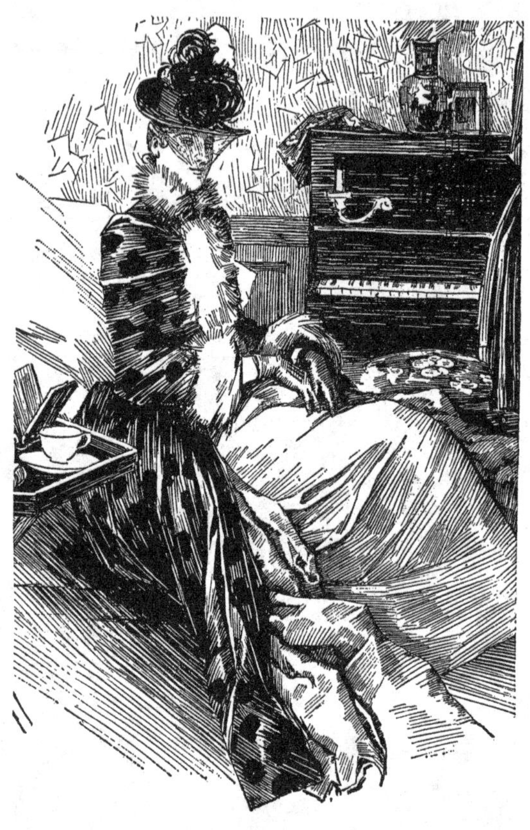

FIG. 16 LESLIE WILLSON

An example of all that is refined and excellent in pen technique is the drawing by Mr. Alfred Brennan, Fig. 15. The student would do well to study this carefully for its marvellous beauty of line. There is little hatching, and yet the tones are deep and rich. The wall tone will be found to be made up similarly to "A" and "H" in Fig. 12. The tone "B" in the same Figure is made up of lines which are thin at the ends and big in the middle, fitting into each other irregularly, and imparting a texture somewhat different from that obtained by the abrupt ending of the strokes of "A." This method is also employed by Brennan, and is a very effective one. A good example of the use of this character of line (unknitted, however) is the drawing by Mr. Leslie Willson, Fig. 16. The irregular line "C" has good possibilities for texture, and the wavy character of "D" is most effective in the rendering of shadows, giving a certain vibration to the atmosphere. "E" and "F" suggest a freer method of rendering a tone; while "G" shows a scribbling line that is sometimes employed to advantage. The very interesting texture of the coat, Fig. 17, is made with a horizontal line having a similar return stroke, as may be noticed where the rendering ends. There are times when an irresponsible sort of line is positively desirable,—say for rough foreground suggestion or for freeing the picture at the edges.

I have invariably found that what presents the chief difficulty to the student of pen and

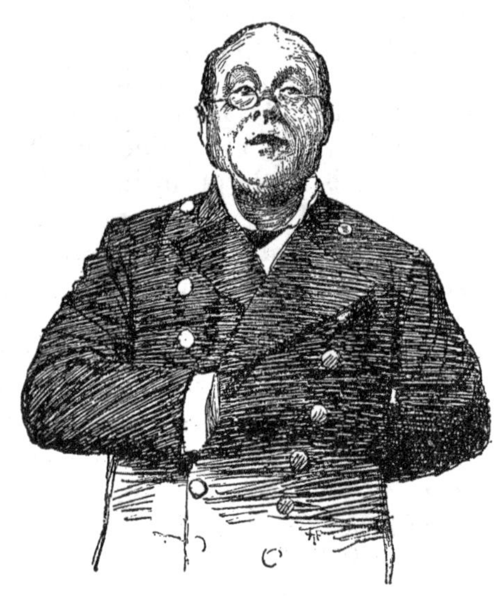

FIG. 17 DRAWING FROM PHOTOGRAPH

From Harper's Magazine, by permission. Copyright, 1892, by Harper & Brothers

ink is the management of the Outline. When it is realized that, by mere outline, one may express the texture of a coat or a tree or a wall without any rendering whatever, it will be seen that nothing in pen drawing is really of so much importance. Notice, for example, the wonderful drawing of the dog in Fig. 34. Again, if a connected line had been used to define the corners of Railton's buttresses in Fig. 7 all the texture would have been de-

Outline

stroyed. Instead of this he has used a broken outline, sometimes omitting it altogether for a considerable space. On the ledges, too, the lines are broken. In Rico's drawing, Fig. 11, all the outlines may be observed to have a break here and there. This broken line is particularly effective in out-door subjects, as it helps to suggest sunlit atmosphere as well as texture.

Architectural outlines, however, are not particularly subtle; it is when we come to render anything with vague boundaries, such as foliage or clouds for example, that the chief difficulties are encountered. Foliage is an important element of landscape drawing and deserves more than passing consideration. To make a successful rendering of a tree in pen and ink the tree must be first well drawn in pencil. It is absolutely impossible to obtain such a charming effect of foliage as that shown in Mr. Pennell's sketch, Fig. 18, without the most painstaking preparation in pencil. The success of this result is not attributable merely to the difference in textures, nor to the direction or character of the line; it is first of all a matter of good drawing. The outline should be free and subtle so as to suggest the edges of leafage, and the holes near the edges should be accented, otherwise they will be lost and the tree will look solid and characterless. Observe, in the same drawing, how

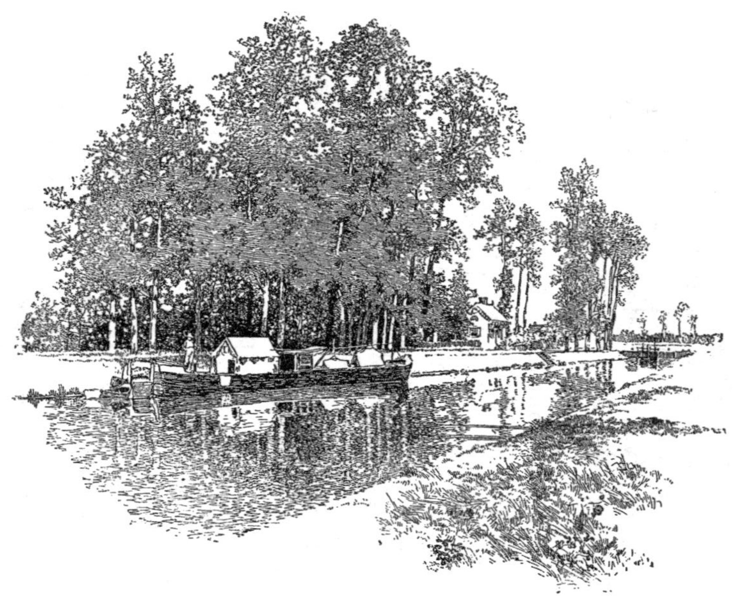

FIG. 18 JOSEPH PENNELL

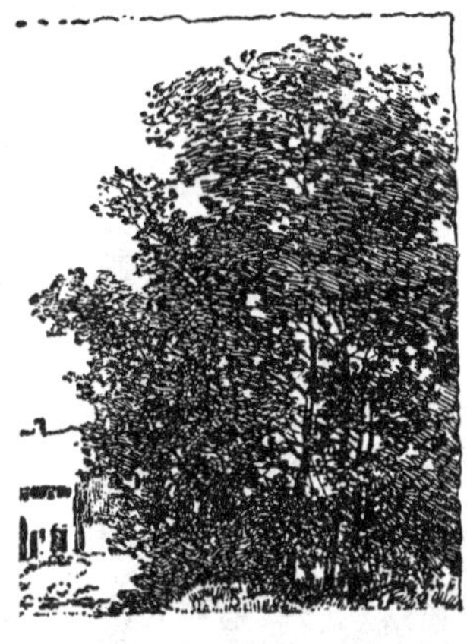

FIG. 19 JOSEPH PENNELL

Mr. Pennell suggests the structure of the leafage by the irregular outlines which he gives to the different series of lines, and which he emphasizes by bringing the lines to an abrupt stop. Observe also how the stronger texture of the tree in Fig. 19 is obtained by making the lines with greater abruptness. Compare both of these Figures with the foreground trees by the same artist in Fig. 20. The last is a brilliant example of foliage drawing in pen and ink.

Textures

The matter of Textures is very important, and the student should learn to differentiate them as much as possible. This is done, as I have already said, by differences in the size and character of the line, and in the closeness or openness of the rendering. Observe the variety of textures in the drawing of the sculptor by Dantan, Fig. 21. The coat is rendered by such a cross-hatch as "N" in Fig. 10, made horizontally and with heavy lines. In the trousers the lines do not cross but fit in

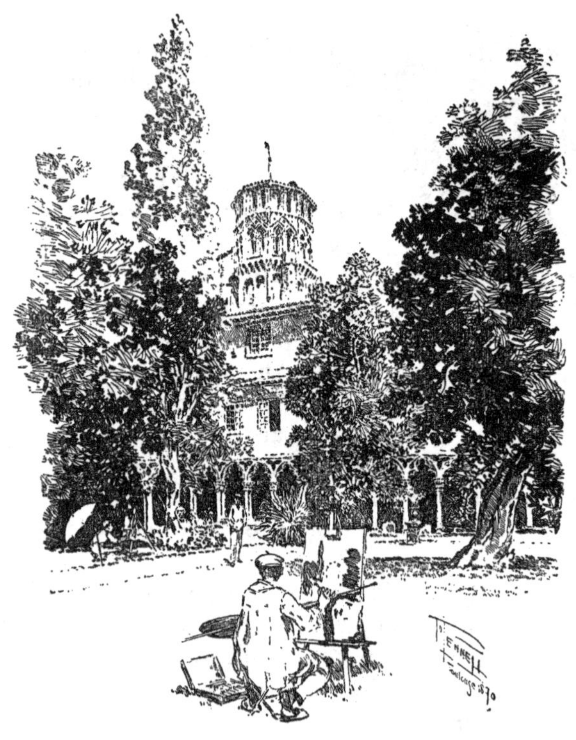

FIG. 20 JOSEPH PENNELL

From Harper's Magazine, by permission. Copyright, 1893, by Harper & Brothers

together. This is an excellent example for study, as is also the portrait by Raffaëlli, Fig. 22. The textures in the latter drawing are wonderfully well conveyed,—the hard, bony face, the stubby beard, and the woolen cap with its tassel in silhouette. For the expression of texture with the least effort the drawings of Vierge are incomparable. The architectural drawing by Mr. Gregg in Fig. 50 is well worth careful study in this connection, as are all of Her-

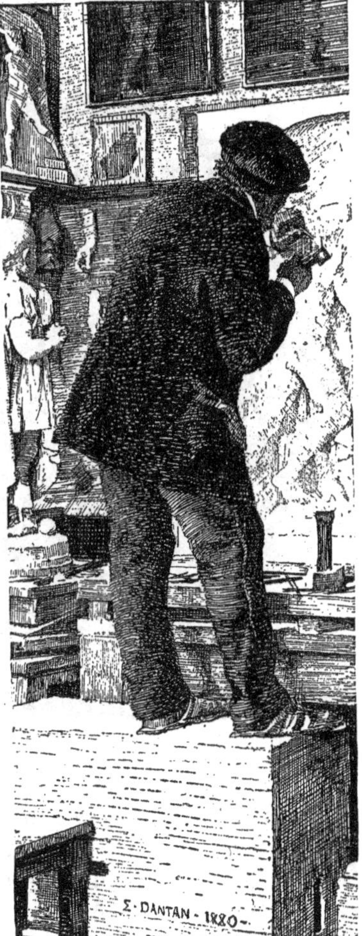

FIG. 21 E. DANTAN

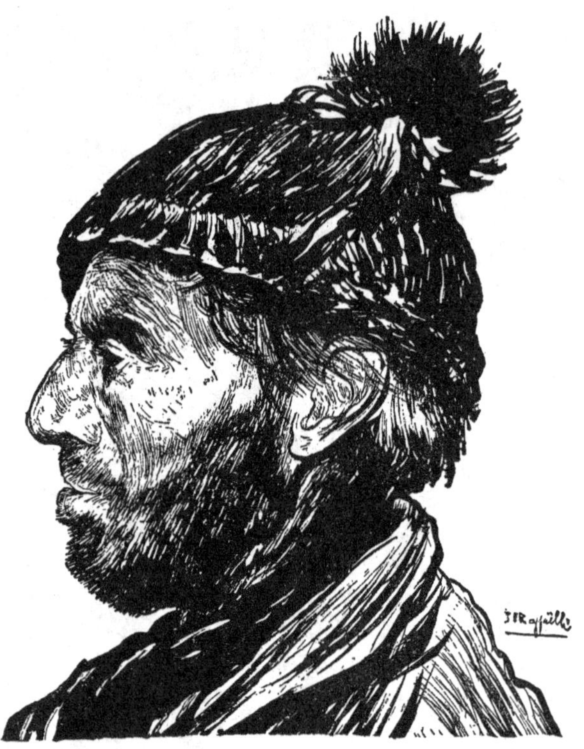

FIG. 22 J. F. RAFFAËLLI

bert Railton's admirable drawings of old English houses. (I recommend the study of Mr. Railton's work with a good deal of reservation, however. While it is admirable in respect of textures and fascinating in its color, the values are likely to be most unreal, and the mannerisms are so pronounced and so tiresome that I regard it as much inferior to that of Mr. Pennell, whose architecture always *appears*, at least, to have been honestly drawn on the spot.)

The hats in Fig. 10 are merely suggestions to the student in the study of elementary combinations of line in expressing textures.

Drawing for Reproduction

As the mechanical processes of Reproduction have much to do with determining pen methods they become important factors for consideration. While their waywardness and inflexibility are the cause of no little distress to the illustrator, the limitations of processes cannot be said, on the whole, to make for inferior standards in drawing, as will be seen by the following rules which they impose, and for which a strict regard will be found most advisable.

First: Make each line clear and distinct. Do not patch up a weak line or leave one which has been broken or blurred by rubbing, for however harmless or even interesting it may seem in your original it will almost certainly be neither in the reproduction. When you make mistakes, erase the offensive part completely, or, if you are working on Bristol-board and the area of unsatisfactoriness be considerable, paste a fresh piece of paper over it and redraw.

Second: Keep your work open. Aim for

economy of line. If a shadow can be rendered with twenty strokes do not crowd in forty, as you will endanger its transparency. Remember that in reproduction the lines tend to thicken and so to crowd out the light between them. This is so distressingly true of newspaper reproduction that in drawings for this purpose the lines have to be generally very thin, sharp, and well apart. The above rule should be particularly regarded in all cases where the drawing is to be subject to much reduction. The degree of reduction of which pen drawings are susceptible is not, as is commonly supposed, subject to rule. It all depends on the scale of the technique.

Third: Have the values few and positive. It is necessary to keep the gray tones pretty distinct to prevent the relation of values being injured, for while the gray tones darken in proportion to the degree of reduction, the blacks cannot, of course, grow blacker. A gray tone which may be light and delicate in the original, will, especially if it be closely knit, darken and thicken in the printing. These rules are most strictly to be observed when drawing for the cheaper classes of publications. For book and magazine work, however, where the plates are touched up by the engraver, and the values in a measure restored, the third rule is not so arbitrary. Nevertheless, the beginner who has ambitions in this direction will do well not to put difficulties in his own way by submitting work not directly printable.

Some Fanciful Expedients

There are a number of more or less fanciful expedients employed in modern pen work which may be noted here, and which are illustrated in Fig. 10. The student is advised, however, to resort to them as little as possible, not only because he is liable to make injudicious use of them, but because it is wiser for him to cultivate the less meretricious possibilities of the instrument.

"Spatter work" is a means of obtaining a delicate printable tone, consisting of innumerable little dots of ink spattered on the paper. The process is as follows: Carefully cover with a sheet of paper all the drawing except the portion which is to be spattered, then take a tooth-brush, moisten the ends of the bristles consistently with ink, hold the brush, back downwards, in the left hand, and with a wooden match or tooth-pick rub the bristles *toward you* so that the ink will spray over the paper. Particular care must be taken that the brush is not so loaded with ink that it will spatter in blots. It is well, therefore, to try it first on a rough sheet of paper, to remove any superfluous ink. If the spattering is well done, it gives a very delicate tone of interesting texture, but if not cleverly employed, and especially if there be a large area of it, it is very likely to look out of character with the line portions of the drawing.

A method sometimes employed to give a soft black effect is to moisten the lobe of the thumb lightly with ink and press it upon the paper. The series of lines of the skin make an impression that can be reproduced by the ordinary line processes. As in the case of spatter work, superfluous ink must be looked after before making the impression so as to avoid leaving hard edges. Thumb markings lend themselves to the rendering of dark smoke, and the like, where the edges require to be soft and vague, and the free direction of the lines impart a feeling of movement.

Interesting effects of texture are sometimes introduced into pen drawings by obtaining the impression of a canvas grain. To produce this, it is necessary that the drawing be made on fairly thin paper. The *modus operandi* is as follows: Place the drawing over a piece of mounted canvas of the desired coarseness of grain, and, holding it firmly, rub a lithographic crayon vigorously over the surface of the paper. The grain of the canvas will be found to be clearly reproduced, and, as the crayon is absolutely black, the effect is capable of reproduction by the ordinary photographic processes.

CHAPTER IV

VALUES

After the subject has been mapped out in pencil, and before beginning the pen work, we have to consider and determine the proper disposition of the Color. By "color" is meant, in this connection, the gamut of values from black to white, as indicated in Fig. 23. The success or failure of the drawing will largely depend upon the disposition of these elements, the quality of the technique being a matter of secondary concern. Beauty of line and texture will not redeem a drawing in which the values are badly disposed, for upon them we depend for the effect of unity, or the pictorial quality. If the values are scattered or patchy the drawing will not focus to any central point of interest, and there will be no unity in the result.

The Color-Scheme

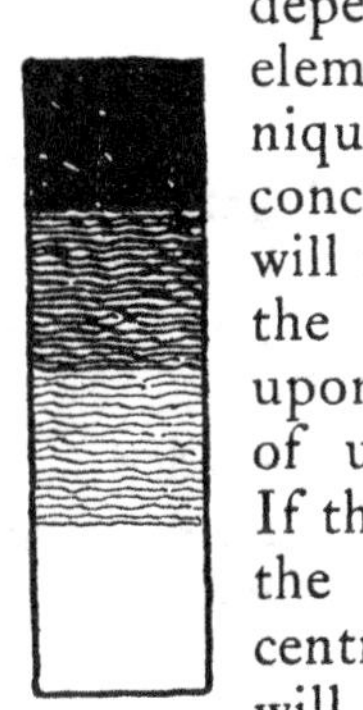

FIG. 23 C.D.M.

There are certain general laws by which color may be pleasingly disposed, but it must be borne in mind that it ought to be disposed naturally as well. By a "natural" scheme of color, I mean one which is consistent with a natural effect of light and shade. Now the gradation from black to white, for example, is a pleasing scheme, as may be observed in Fig. 24, yet the effect is unnatural, since the sky is black. In a purely decorative illustration like this, however, such logic need not be considered.

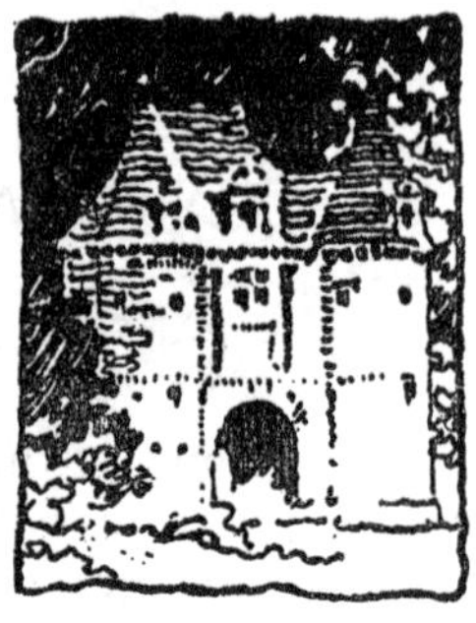

FIG. 24 D. A. GREGG

Principality in the Color-Scheme

Since, as I said before, color is the factor which makes for the unity of the result, the first principle to be regarded in its arrangement is that of Principality,—there must be some dominant note in the rendering. There should not, for instance, be two principal dark spots of equal value in the same drawing, nor two equally prominent areas of white. The Vierge drawing, Fig. 25, and that by Mr. Pennell, Fig. 5, are no exceptions to this rule; the black figure of the old man counting as one note in the former, as do the dark arches of the bridge in the latter. The work of both these artists is eminently worthy of study for the knowing manner in which they dispose their values.

Variety

The next thing to be sought is Variety. Too obvious or positive a scheme, while possibly not unsuitable for a conventional decorative drawing, may not be well adapted to a

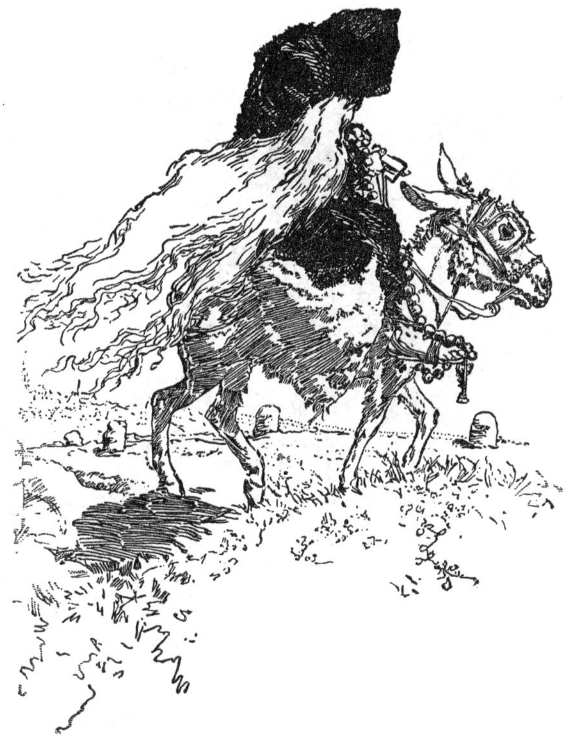

FIG. 25 DANIEL VIERGE

perspective subject. The large color areas should be echoed by smaller ones throughout the picture. Take, for example, the Vierge drawing shown in Fig. 26. Observe how the mass of shadow is relieved by the two light holes seen through the inn door. Without

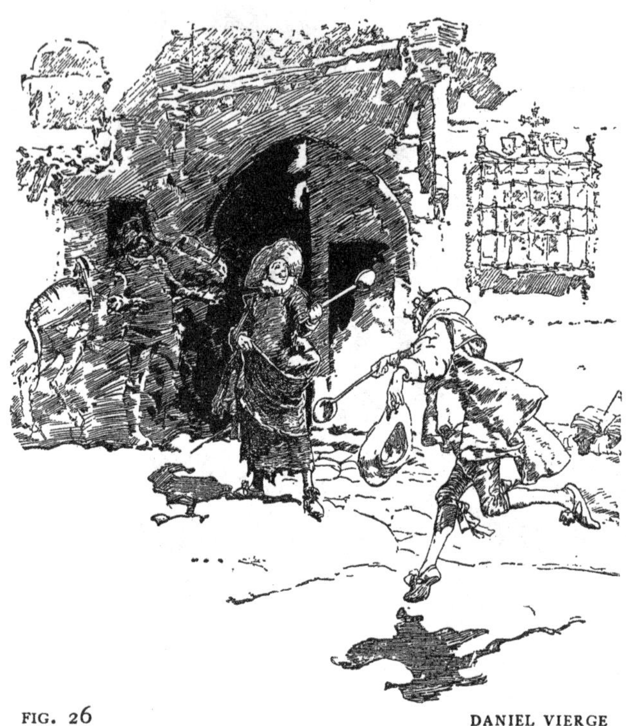

FIG. 26 DANIEL VIERGE

this repetition of the white the drawing would lose much of its character. In Rico's drawing, Fig. 11, a tiny white spot in the shadow cast over the street would, I venture to think, be helpful, beautifully clear as it is; and the black area at the end of the wall seems a defect as it competes in value with the dark figure.

Lastly, Breadth of Effect has to be considered. It is requisite that, however numerous the tones are (and they should not be too numerous), the general effect should be simple and homogeneous. The color must count together broadly, and not be cut up into patches.

Breadth of Effect

It is important to remember that the gamut from black to white is a short one for the pen. One need only try to faithfully render the high lights of an ordinary table glass set against a gray background, to be assured of its limitations in this respect. To represent even approximately the subtle values would require so much ink that nothing short of a positively black background would suffice to give a semblance of the delicate transparent effect of the glass as a whole. The gray background would, therefore, be lost, and if a really black object were also part of the picture it could not be rep-

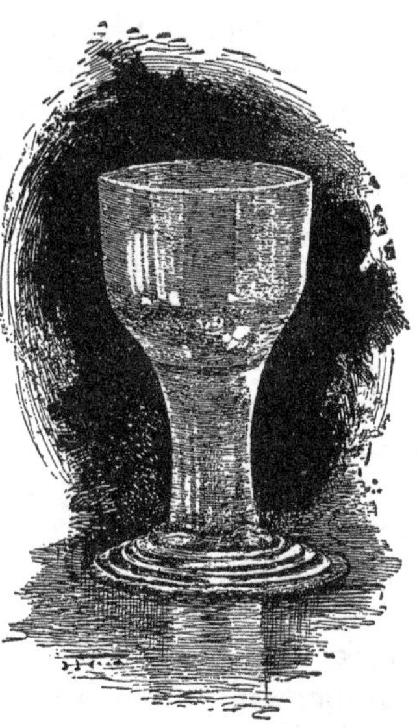

FIG. 27 HARRY FENN

resented at all. Observe, in Fig. 27, how just such a problem has been worked out by Mr. Harry Fenn.

It will be manifest that the student must learn to think of things in their broad relation. To be specific,—in the example just considered, in order to introduce a black object the scheme of color would have needed broadening so that the gray background could be given its proper value, thus demanding that the elaborate values of the glass be ignored, and just enough suggested to give the general effect. This reasoning would equally apply were the light object, instead of a glass, something of intricate design, presenting positive shadows. Just so much of such a design should be rendered as not to darken the object below its proper relative value as a whole. In this faculty of suggesting things without literally rendering them consists the subtlety of pen drawing.

It may be said, therefore, that large light areas resulting from the necessary elimination of values are characteristic of pen drawing. The degree of such elimination depends, of course, upon the character of the subject, this being entirely a matter of relation. The more black there is in a drawing the greater the number of values that can be represented. Generally speaking, three or four are all that can be managed, and the beginner had better

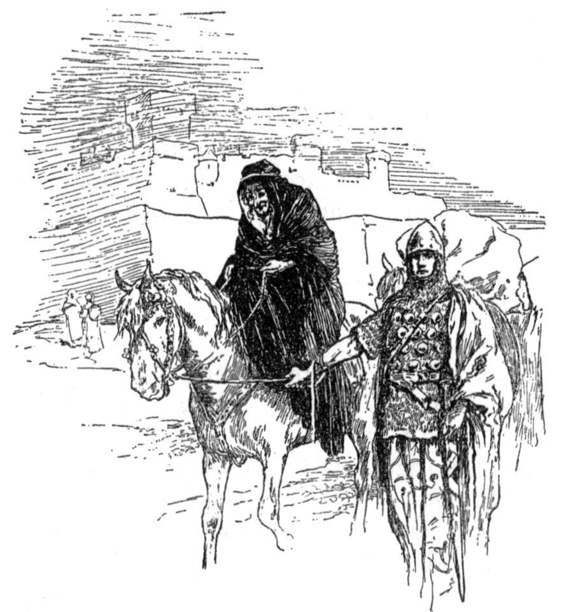

FIG. 28 REGINALD BIRCH

get along with three,—black, half-tone, and white.

Various Color-Schemes

While it is true that every subject is likely to contain some motive or suggestion for its appropriate color-scheme, it still holds that, many times, and especially in those cases where the introduction of foreground features at considerable scale is necessary for the interest of the picture, an artificial arrangement has to be devised. It is well, therefore, to be acquainted with the possibilities of certain color combinations. The most brilliant effect in black and white drawing is that obtained by placing the prominent black against a white area surrounded by gray. The white shows whiter because of the gray around it, so that the contrast of the black against it is extremely vigorous and telling. This may be said to be the illustrator's *tour de force*. We have it illustrated by Mr. Reginald Birch's drawing, Fig. 28. Observe how the contrast of black and white is framed in by the gray made up of the sky, the left side of the building, the horse, and the knight. In the drawing by Mr. Pennell, Fig. 29, we have the same scheme of color. Notice how the trees are darkest just where they are required to tell most strongly against the white in the centre of the picture. An admirable illustration of the effectiveness of this color-scheme is shown in the "Becket" poster by the "Beggarstaff Brothers," Fig. 69. Another scheme is to have the principal black in the gray area, as in the Vierge drawing, Fig. 26, and in Rico's sketch, Fig. 11.

Still another and a more restful scheme is the actual gradation of color. This gradation, from black to white, wherein the white occupies the centre of the picture, is to be noted in Fig. 20. Observe how the dark side of the foreground tree tells against the light side of the one beyond, which, in its turn, is yet so strongly shaded as to count brilliantly against

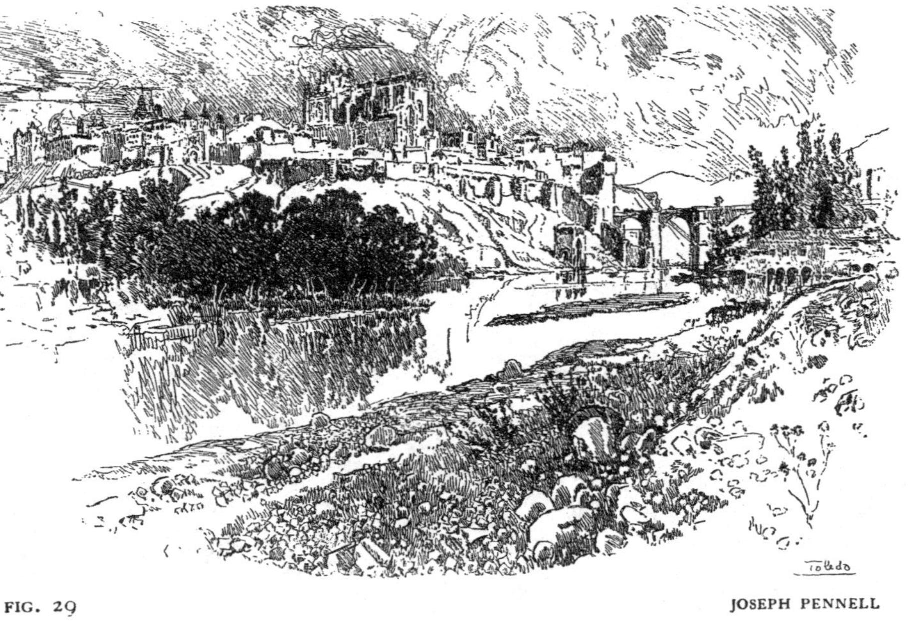

FIG. 29 JOSEPH PENNELL

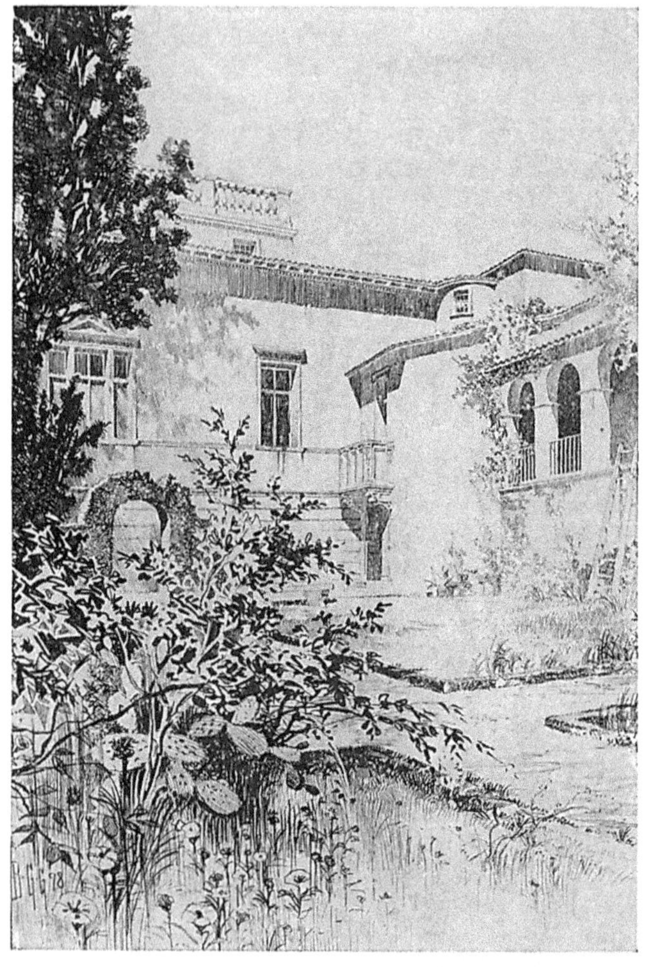

FIG. 30 B. G. GOODHUE

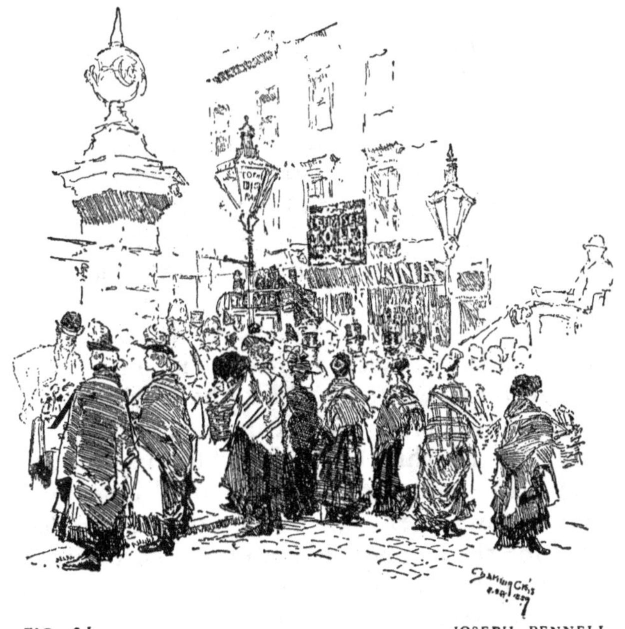

FIG. 31 JOSEPH PENNELL

the white building. Still again, in Mr. Goodhue's drawing, Fig. 30, note how the transition from the black tree on the left to the white building is pleasingly softened by the gray shadow. Notice, too, how the brilliancy of the drawing is heightened by the gradual emphasis on the shadows and the openings as they approach the centre of the picture. Yet another example of this color-scheme is the drawing by Mr. Gregg, Fig. 50. The gradation here is from the top of the picture downwards. The sketch of the coster women by Mr. Pennell, Fig. 31, shows this gradation reversed.

The drawing of the hansom cab, Fig. 32, by Mr. Raven Hill, illustrates a very strong color-scheme,—gray and white separated by black, the gray moderating the black on the upper side, leaving it to tell strongly against the white below. Notice how luminous is this same relation of color where it occurs in the Venetian subject by Rico, Fig. 14. The shadow on the water qualifies the blackness of the gondola below, permitting a brilliant contrast with the white walls of the building above.

It is interesting to observe how Vierge and Pennell, but chiefly the former, very often depend for their grays merely upon the delicate tone resulting from the rendering of form and of direct shadow, without any local color. This may be seen in the Vierge drawing, Fig. 33. Observe in this, as a consequence, how brilliantly the tiny black counts in the little figure in the centre. Notice, too, in the drawing of the soldiers by Jeanniot, Fig. 34, that there is very little black; and yet see how brilliant is the effect, owing largely to the figures being permitted to stand out against a white ground in which nothing is indicated but the sky-line of the large building in the distance.

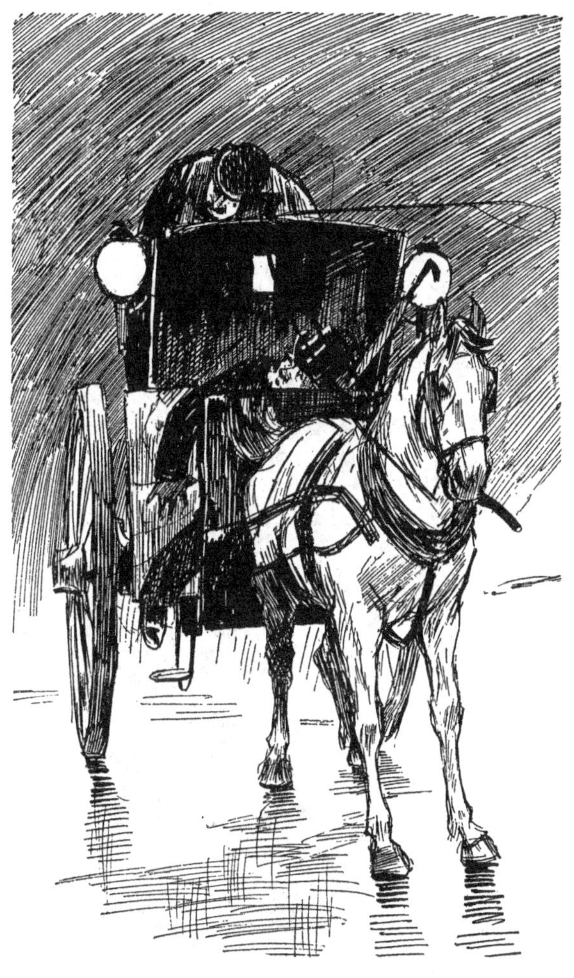

FIG. 32 L. RAVEN HILL

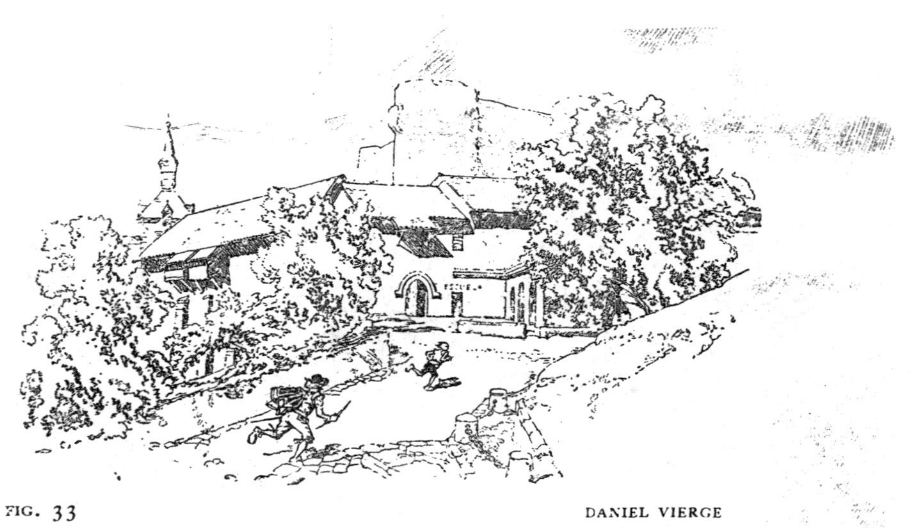

FIG. 33 DANIEL VIERGE

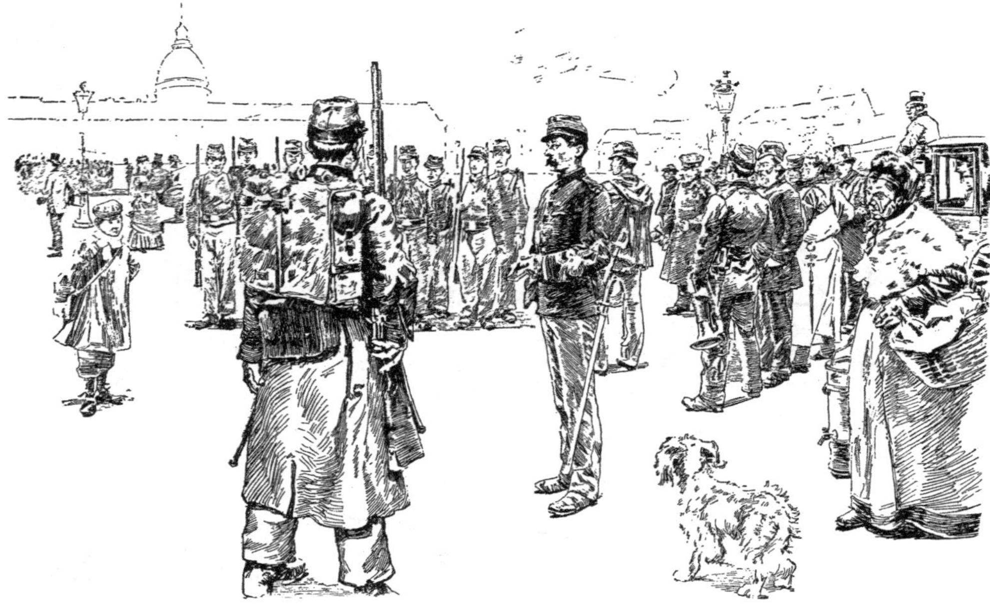

FIG. 34 P. G. JEANNIOT

CHAPTER V

PRACTICAL PROBLEMS

I have thought it advisable in this chapter to select, and to work out in some detail, a few actual problems in illustration, so as to familiarize the student with the practical application of some of the principles previously laid down.

First Problem In the first example the photograph, Fig. 35, shows the porch of an old English country church. Let us see how this subject has been interpreted in pen and ink by Mr. D. A. Gregg, Fig. 36. In respect to the lines, the original composition presents nothing essentially unpleasant. Where the strong accent of a picture occurs in the centre, however, it is generally desirable to avoid much

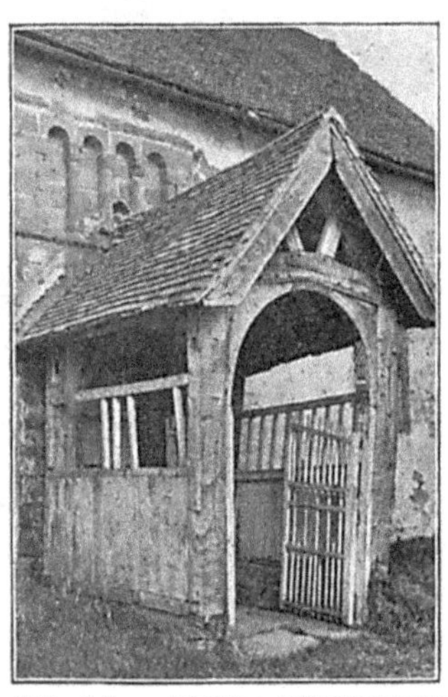

FIG. 35 FROM A PHOTOGRAPH

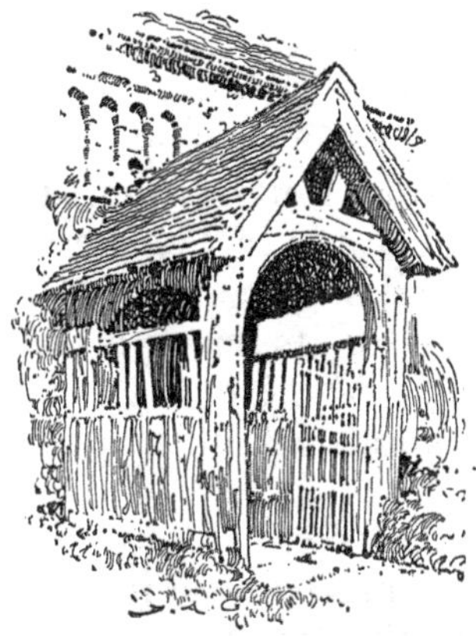

FIG. 36 D. A. GREGG

emphasis at the edges. For this reason the pen drawing has been "vignetted," — that is to say, permitted to fade away irregularly at the edges. Regarding the values, it will be seen that there is no absolute white in the photograph. A literal rendering of such low color would, as we saw in the preceding chapter, be out of the question; and so the essential values which directly contribute to the expression of the subject and which are independent of local color or accidental effect have to be sought out. We observe, then, that the principal note of the photograph is made by the dark part of the roof under the porch relieved against the light wall beyond. This is the direct result of light and shade, and is therefore logically adopted as the principal note of Mr. Gregg's sketch also. The wall at this point is made perfectly white to heighten the contrast. To still further increase the light area, the upper part of the porch has been left almost white, the markings suggesting the construction of the weather-beaten timber serving to give it a faint gray tone sufficient to relieve it from the white wall. The low color of the grass, were it rendered literally, would make the drawing too heavy and uninteresting, and this is therefore only suggested in the sketch. The roof of the main building, being equally objectionable on account of its mass of low tone, is similarly treated. Mr. Gregg's excellent handling of the old woodwork of the porch is well worthy of study.

Second Problem

Let us take another example. The photograph in Fig. 37 shows a moat-house in Normandy; and, except that the low tones of the foliage are exaggerated by the camera, the conditions are practically those which we would have to consider were we making a sketch on the spot. First of all, then, does the subject, from the point of view at which the photograph is taken, compose well?* It cannot be said that it does. The vertical lines made by the two towers are unpleasantly emphasized by the trees behind them. The tree on the left were much better reduced in height and placed somewhat to the right, so that the top should fill out the awkward angles of the roof formed by the junction of the tower and the main building. The trees on the right might be lowered also, but otherwise permitted to retain their present relation. The growth of ivy on the

The student is advised to consult "Composition," by Arthur W. Dow. [New York, 1898.]

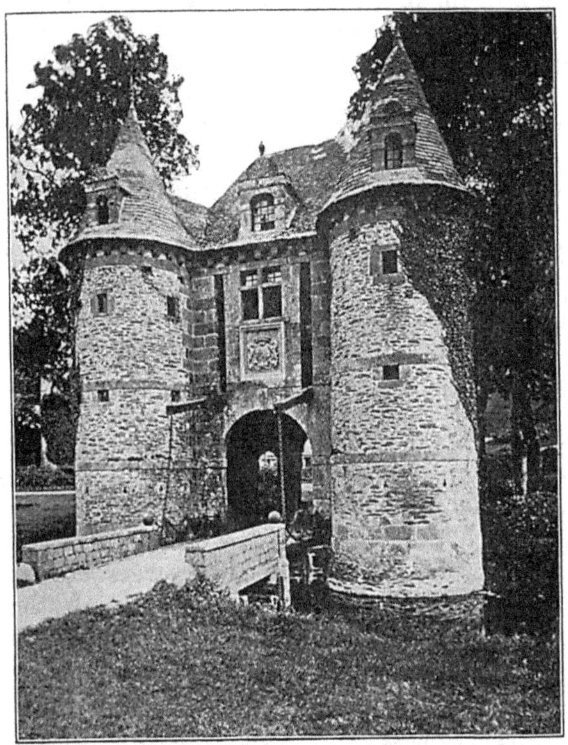

FIG. 37 FROM A PHOTOGRAPH

tower takes an ugly outline, and might be made more interestingly irregular in form.

The next consideration is the disposition of the values. In the photograph the whites are confined to the roadway of the bridge and the bottom of the tower. This is evidently due, however, to local color rather than to the direction of the light, which strikes the nearer tower from the right, the rest of the walls being in shadow. While the black areas of the picture are large enough to carry a mass of gray without sacrificing the sunny look, such a scheme would be likely to produce a labored effect. Two alternative schemes readily suggest themselves: First, to make the archway the principal dark, the walls light, with a light half-tone for the roof, and a darker effect for the trees on the right. Or, second, to make these trees themselves the principal dark, as suggested by the photograph, allowing them to count against the gray of the roof and the ivy of the tower. This latter scheme is that which has been adopted in the sketch, Fig. 38.

It will be noticed that the trees are not nearly so dark as in the photograph. If they were, they would be overpowering in so large an area of white. It was thought better, also, to change the direction of the light, so that the dark ivy, instead of acting contradictorily to the effect, might lend character to the shaded side. The lower portion of the nearer tower was toned in, partly to qualify the vertical line of the tower, which would have been unpleasant if the shading were uniform, and partly to carry the gray around to the entrance. It was thought advisable, also, to cut from the

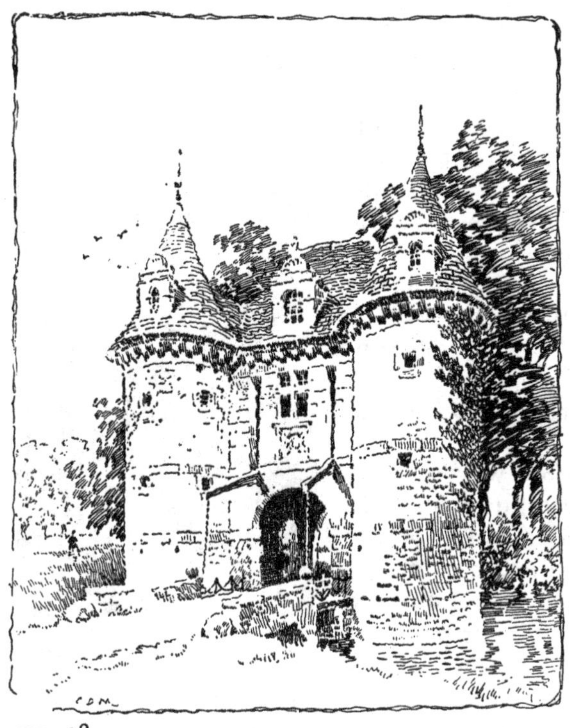

FIG. 38 C. D. M.

foreground, raising the upper limit of the picture correspondingly. (It is far from my intention, however, to convey the impression that any liberties may be taken with a subject in order to persuade it into a particular scheme of composition; and in this very instance an artistic photographer could probably have discovered a position for his camera which would have obviated the necessity for any change whatever;—a nearer view of the building, for one thing, would have considerably lowered the trees.)

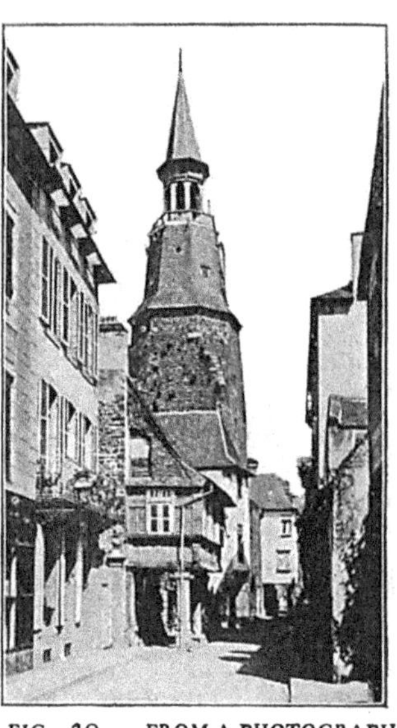

FIG. 39 FROM A PHOTOGRAPH

Third Problem

We will consider still another subject. The photograph, Fig. 39, shows a street in Holland. In this case, the first thing we have to determine is where the interest of the subject centres. In such a perspective the salient point of the picture often lies in a foreground building; or, if the street be merely a setting for the representation of some incident, in a group of foreground figures. In either case the emphasis should be placed in the foreground, the distant vanishing lines of the street being rendered more or less vaguely. In the present subject, however, the converging sky and street lines are broken by the quaint clock-tower. This and the buildings underneath it appeal to us at once as the most important elements of the picture. The nearer buildings present nothing intrinsically interesting, and therefore serve no better purpose than to lead the eye to the centre of interest. Whatever actual values these intermediate buildings have that will hinder their usefulness in this regard can, therefore, be changed or actually ignored without affecting the integrity of the sketch or causing any pangs of conscience.

The building on the extreme left shows very strong contrasts of color in the black shadow of the eaves and of the shop-front below. These contrasts, coming as they do at the edge of the picture, are bad. They would act like a showy frame on a delicate drawing, keeping the eye from the real subject. It may be objected, however, that it is natural that the contrasts should be stronger in the foreground. Yes; but in looking straight at the clock-tower one does not see any such dark shadow at the top of the very uninteresting building in the left foreground. The camera saw it, because the camera with its hundred eyes sees everything, and does not interest itself about any one thing in particular. Besides, if the keeper of the shop had the bad taste to paint it dark we are not bound to make a record of the fact; nor need we assume that it was done out of regard to the pictorial possibilities of the street. We decide, therefore, to render, as faithfully as we may, the values of the clock-tower and its immediate surroundings, and to disregard the discordant elements ; and we have no hesitation in selecting for principal emphasis in our drawing, Fig. 40, the shadow under the projecting building. This dark accent will count brilliantly against the foreground and the walls of the buildings, which we will treat broadly as if white, ignoring the slight differences in value shown in the photograph. We retain, however, the literal values of the clock-tower and the buildings underneath it, and express as nearly as we can their interesting variations of texture. The buildings on the right are too black in the photograph, and these, as well as the shadow thrown across the street, we will considerably lighten. After some experiment, we find that the building on the extreme left is a nuisance, and we omit it. Even then, the one with the balcony next to it requires to be toned down in its strong values, and so the shadows here are made much lighter, the walls being kept white. It will be found that anything like a strong emphasis of the projecting eaves of the building would detract from the effect of the tower, so that the shadow under the eaves is, therefore, made grayer than in the photograph, while that of the balcony below is made stronger than the shadow of the eaves, but is lightened at the edge of the drawing to throw the emphasis toward the centre.

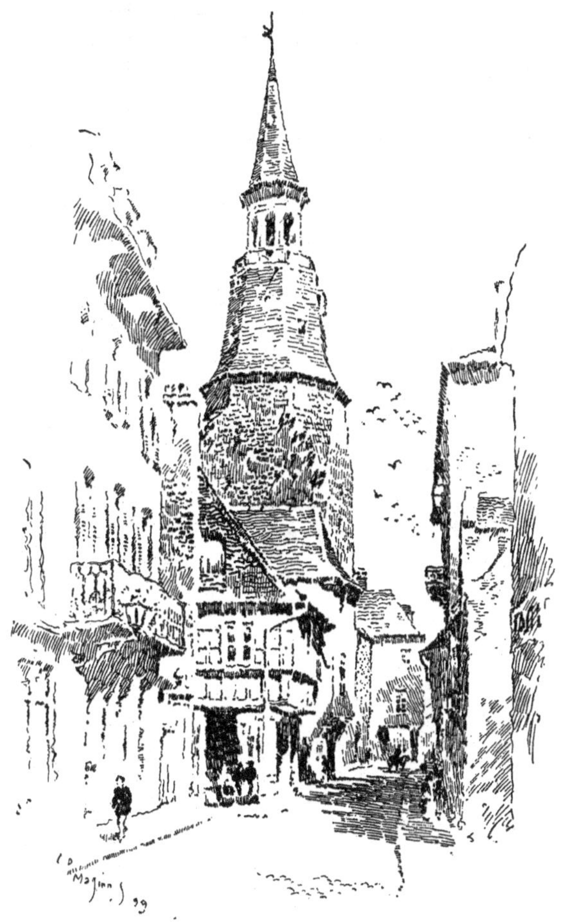

FIG. 40 C. D. M.

To add interest to the picture, and more especially to give life to the shadows, several figures are introduced. It will be noticed that the cart is inserted at the focal point of the drawing to better assist the perspective.

CHAPTER VI

ARCHITECTURAL DRAWING

It is but a few years since architects' perspectives were "built up" (it would be a mistake to say "drawn") by means of a T-square and the ruling pen; and if architectural drawing has not quite kept pace with that for general illustration since, a backward glance over the professional magazines encourages a feeling of comparative complacency. That so high a standard or so artistic a character is not observable in architectural as in general illustration is, I think, not difficult to explain. Very few of the clever architectural draughtsmen are illustrators by profession. Few, even of those who are generally known as illustrators, are anything more — I should perhaps say anything *less* — than versatile architects; and yet Mr. Pennell, who would appear to assume, in his book on drawing, that the point of view of the architect is normally pictorial, seems at a loss to explain why Mr. Robert Blum, for instance, can illustrate an architectural subject more artistically than any of the draughtsmen in the profession. Without accepting his premises, it is remarkably creditable to architecture that it counts among its members in this country such men as Mr. B. G. Goodhue and Mr. Wilson Eyre, Jr., and in England such thorough artists as Mr. Prentice and Mr. Ernest George — men known even to distinction for their skill along lines of purely architectural practice, yet any one of whom would, I venture to say, cause considerable displacement did he invade the ranks of magazine illustrators. Moreover (and the suggestion is not unkindly offered), were the architects and the illustrators to change places architecture would suffer most by the process.

The Architects' Case

That the average architect should be incapable of artistically illustrating his own design, ought, I think, to be less an occasion for surprise than that few painters, whose point of view is essentially pictorial, can make even a tolerable interpretation in line of their own paintings. Be it remembered that the pictures made by the architect are seldom the records of actualities. The buildings themselves are merely contemplated, and the illustrations are worked up from geometrical elevations in the office, very, very far from Nature. Moreover, the subjects are not infrequently such as lend themselves with an ill grace to picturesque illustration. The structure to be depicted may, for instance, be a heavy cubical mass with a bald uninteresting sky-line; or it may be a tall office building, impossible to reconcile with natural accessories either in pictorial scale or in composition. These natural accessories, too, the draughtsman must, with an occasional recourse to his photograph album, evolve out of his inner consciousness. When it is further considered that such structures, even when actualities, are uncompromisingly stiff and immaculate in their newness, presenting absolutely none of those interesting accidents so dear to the artist, and perhaps with nothing whatever about them of picturesque suggestion, we have a problem presented which is somewhat analogous to that presented by the sculpturesque possibilities of "fashionable trousering." That, with such uninspiring conditions, architectural illustration does not develop so interesting a character nor attain to so high a standard as distinguishes general illustration is not to be wondered at. It is rather an occasion for surprise that it exhibits so little of the artificiality of the fashion-plate after all, and that the better part of it, at least, is not more unworthy than figure illustration would be were it denied the invaluable aid of the living model. So much by way of apology.

The Architects' Point of View

The architectural perspective, however, is not to be regarded purely from the pictorial point of view. It is an illustration first, a picture afterwards, and almost invariably deals with an individual building, which is the essential subject. This building cannot, therefore, be made a mere foil for interesting "picturesqueries," nor subordinated to any scenic effect of landscape or chiaroscuro. Natural accessories or interesting bits of street life may be added to give it an appropriate setting; but the result must clearly read "Building, with landscape," not "Landscape, with building."

Much suggestion for the sympathetic handling of particular subjects may be found in the character of the architecture itself. The illustrator ought to enter into the spirit of the designer, ought to feel just what natural accessories lend themselves most harmoniously to this or that particular type. If the architecture be quaint and picturesque it must not have prosaic surroundings. If, on the other hand, it be formal or monumental, the character and scale of the accessories should be accordingly serious and dignified. The rendering ought also to vary with the subject,—a free picturesque manner for the one, a more studied and responsible handling for the other. Technique is the language of art, and a stiff pompous phraseology will accord ill with a story of quaint humor or pathos, while the homely diction that might answer very well would be sure to struggle at a disadvantage with the stately meanings and diplomatic subtleties of a state document.

Rendering of Detail

It would be well for the student, before venturing upon whole subjects, to learn to render details, such as windows, cornices, etc. Windows are a most important feature of the architectural drawing, and the beginner must study them carefully, experimenting for the method which will best represent their glassy surfaces. No material gives such play of light and shade as glass does. One window is never absolutely like another; so that while a certain uniformity in their value may be required for breadth of effect in the drawing of a building, there is plenty of opportunity for incidental variety in their treatment.

A few practical hints on the rendering of windows may prove serviceable. Always emphasize the sash. Where there is no recess, as in wooden buildings, strengthen the inner line of sash, as in Fig. 41. In masonry buildings the frame and sash can be given their proper values, the area of wood being treated broadly, without regard to the individual members. The wood may, however, be left white if required, as would be the case in Colonial designs. In either case the dark shadow which the sash casts on the glass should be suggested, if the scale of the drawing be such as to permit of it. Do not try to show too much. One is apt to make a fussy effect, if, for instance, one insists on always shading the soffit of the masonry opening, especially if the scale of the drawing be small. Besides, a white soffit is not a false but merely a forced value, as in strong sunlight the reflected light is considerable. If the frame be left white, however, the soffit ought to be shaded, otherwise it will be difficult to keep the values distinct. In respect of wooden buildings there is no need to always complete the mouldings of the architrave. Notice in Fig. 41 that, in the window without the muntins, the mouldings have been carried round the top to give color, but that in the other they are merely suggested at the corners so as to avoid confusion. Care should be taken to avoid mechanical rendering of the muntins. For the glass itself, a uniformly flat tone is to be avoided. The tones should soften vaguely. It will be found, too, that it is not advisable to have a strong dark effect at the top of the window and another at the bottom; one should predominate.

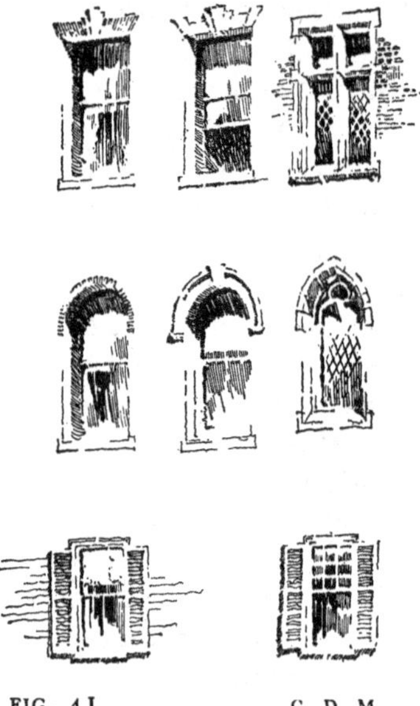

FIG. 41 C. D. M.

The student after careful study of Fig. 41 should make from it enlarged drawings, and afterwards, laying the book aside, proceed to render them in his own way. When he has done so, let him compare his work with the originals. This process ought to be repeated several times, the aim being always for *similarity*, not for *literalness* of effect. If he can get equally good results with another method he need not be disconcerted at the lack of any further resemblance.

The cornice with its shadow is another salient feature. In short shadows, such as those cast by cornices, it is well, if a sunny effect be desired, to accent the bottom edge of the shadow. The shadow lines ought to be generally parallel, but with enough variation to obviate a mechanical effect. They need not be vertical lines,—in fact it is better that they should take the same slant as the light. If they are not absolutely perpendicular, however, it is well to make them distinctly oblique, otherwise the effect will be unpleasant. A clever sketch of a cornice by Mr. George F. Newton is shown in Fig. 42. Notice how well the texture of the brick is expressed by the looseness of the pen work. Some of the detail, too, is dexterously handled, notably the bead and button moulding.

The strength of the cornice shadow should be determined by the tone of the roof above it. To obtain for this shadow the very distinct value which it ought to have, however, does not require that the roof be kept always much lighter than it. In the gable roof in Fig. 57, the tone of the roof is shaded lighter as it approaches the eaves, so that the shadow may count more emphatically. This order may be reversed, as in the case of a building with dark roof and light walls, in which case the shadow may be grayer than the lower portion of the roof, as in "B" in Fig. 44.

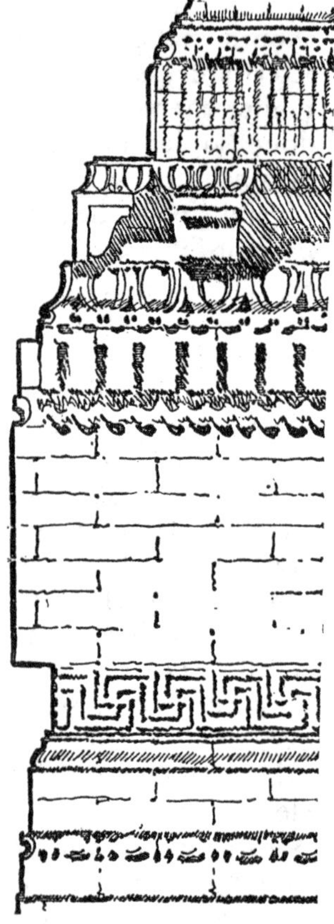

FIG. 42 GEORGE F. NEWTON

But the beginner should not yet hurry on to whole subjects. A church porch, as in Fig. 35, or a dormer with its shadow cast on a roof, as in Fig. 43, will be just as beneficial a study for him as an entire building, and will afford quite as good an opportunity for testing his knowledge of the principles of pen drawing, with the added advantage that either of the subjects mentioned can be mapped out in a few minutes, and that a failure or two, therefore, will not prove so discouraging as if a more intricate subject had to be re-drawn. I have known promising beginners to give up pen and ink drawing in despair because they found themselves unequal to subjects which would have presented not a few difficulties to the experienced illustrator. When the beginner grows faint-hearted, let him seek consolation and encouragement in the thought that were pen drawing something to be mastered in a week or a month there would be small merit in the accomplishment.

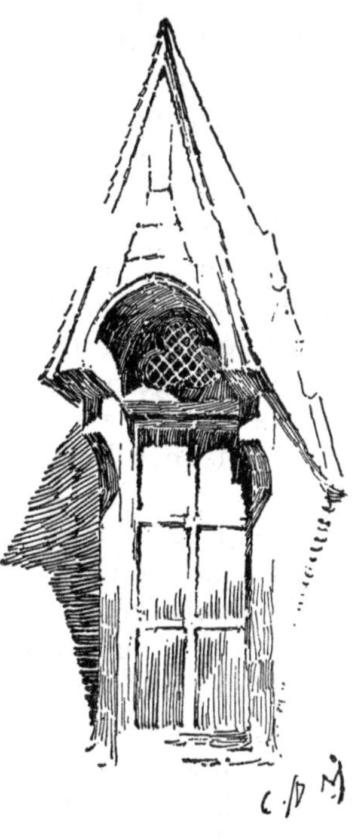

FIG. 43 C. D. M.

It is a common fault of students to dive

into the picture unthinkingly, beginning anywhere, without the vaguest plan of a general effect, whereas it is of the utmost importance that every stroke of the pen be made with intelligent regard to the ultimate result. The following general method will be found valuable.

A General System

Pencil the outline of the entire subject before beginning the pen work. It will not do to start on the rendering as soon as the building alone is pencilled out, leaving the accessories to be put in as one goes along. The adjacent buildings, the foliage, and even the figures must be drawn — carefully drawn — before the pen is taken up. The whole subject from the very beginning should be under control, and to that end it becomes necessary to have all the elements of it pre-arranged.

Arrangement of the Values

Next scheme out the values. This is the time to do the thinking. Do not start out rashly as soon as everything is outlined in pencil, confident in the belief that all windows, for instance, are dark, and that you may as well make them so at once and be done with them. This will be only to court disaster. Besides, all windows are not dark; they may be very light indeed. The color value of nothing is absolute. A shadow may seem almost black till a figure passes into it, when it may become quite gray by comparison. So a window with the sun shining full upon it, or even one in shade, on which a reflected light is cast, may be brilliantly light until the next instant a cloud shadow is reflected in it, making it densely black. Arrange the values, therefore, with reference to one general effect, deciding first of all on the direction of the light. Should this be such as to throw large areas of shadow, these masses of gray will be important elements in the color-scheme. An excellent way to study values is to make a tracing-paper copy of the line drawing and to experiment on this for the color with charcoal, making several sketches if necessary. After having determined on a satisfactory scheme, put fixatif on the rough sketch and keep it in sight. Otherwise, one is liable, especially if the subject is an intricate one, to be led astray by little opportunities for interesting effects here and there, only to discover, when too late, that these effects do not hang together and that the drawing has lost its breadth. The rough sketch is to the draughtsman what manuscript notes are to the lecturer.

Treatment of Detail

Do not be over-conscious of detail. It is a common weakness of the architectural draughtsman to be too sophisticated in his pictorial illustration. He knows so much about the building that no matter how many thousand yards away from it he may stand he will see things that would not reveal themselves to another with the assistance of a field-glass. He is conscious of the fact that there are just so many brick courses to the foot, that the clapboards are laid just so many inches to the weather, that there are just so many mouldings in the belt course, — that everything in general is very, very mathematical. This is not because his point of view is too big, but because it is too small. He who sees so much never by any chance sees the *whole building*. Let him try to think broadly of things. Even should he succeed in forgetting some of these factitious details, the result will still be stiff enough, so hard is it to re-adjust one's attitude after manipulating the T-square. I strongly recommend, as an invaluable aid toward such a re-adjustment, the habit of sketching from Nature, — from the figure during the winter evenings, and out of doors in summer.

The beginner is apt to find his effects at first rather hard and mechanical at the best, because he has not yet attained that freedom of handling which ignores unimportant details, suggests rather than states, gives interesting variations of line and tone, and differentiates textures. A good part of the unpleasantness of effect will undoubtedly be found to be due to a mistaken regard for accuracy of statement, individual mouldings being lined in as deliberately as in the geometrical office drawings, and not an egg nor a dart slighted. Take, for example, the case of an old Colonial building with its white cornice, or any building with white trimmings. See the effect of such a one in an "elevation" where all the detail is drawn, as in "A," Fig. 44. Observe that the amount of ink neces-

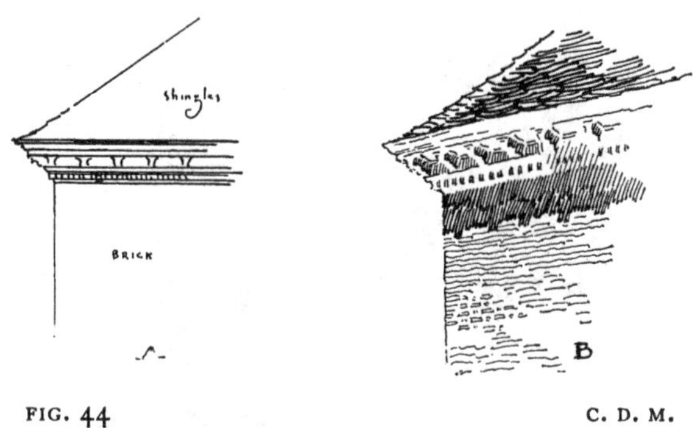

FIG. 44 C. D. M.

sary to express this detail has made the cornice darker than the rest of the drawing, and yet this is quite the reverse of the value which it would have in the actual building, see "B." To obtain the true value the different mouldings which make up the cornice should be merely suggested. Where it is not a question of local color, however, this matter of elimination is largely subject to the exigencies of reproduction; the more precisely and intimately one attempts to render detail, the smaller the scale of the technique requires to be, and the

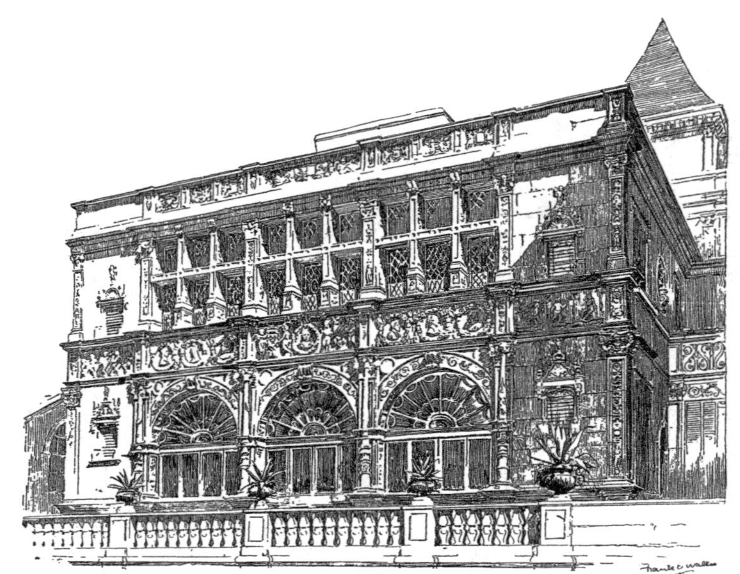

FIG. 45 FRANK E. WALLIS

greater the difficulty. Consequently, the more the reduction which the drawing is likely to undergo in printing, the more one will be obliged to disregard the finer details. These finer details need not, however, be absolutely ignored. Notice, for instance, the clever suggestion of the sculpture in the admirable drawing by Mr. F. E. Wallis, Fig. 45. The conventional drawing of the façade, Fig. 46, is a fine illustration of the decorative effect of color obtainable by emphasizing the organic lines of the design.

Foliage and Figures

The elements in a perspective drawing which present most difficulties to the architectural draughtsman are foliage and figures. These are, however, most important accessories, and must be cleverly handled. It is difficult to say which is the harder to draw, a tree or a human figure; and if the student has not sketched much from Nature either will prove a stumbling-block. Presuming, therefore, that he has already filled a few sketch-books, he had better resort to these, or to his photograph album, when he needs figures for his perspective. Designing figures and trees out of one's inner consciousness is slow work and not very profitable; and if the figure draughtsman may employ models, the architect may be permitted to use photographs.

Unhappily for the beginner, no two illustrators consent to render foliage, or anything

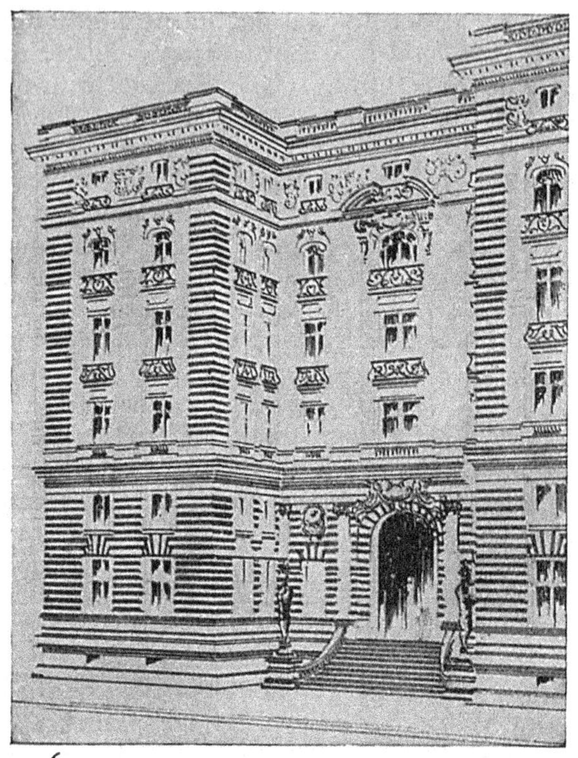

FIG. 46 HARRY ALLAN JACOBS

else for that matter, in quite the same way, and so I cannot present any authoritative formula for doing so. This subject has been treated, however, in a previous chapter, and nothing need be added here except to call attention to an employment of foliage peculiar to architectural drawings. This is the broad suggestive rendering of dark leafage at the sides of a building, to give it relief. The example shown in Fig. 47 is from one of Mr. Gregg's drawings.

The rendering of the human figure need not be dealt with under this head, as figures in an architectural subject are of necessity relatively small, and therefore have to be rendered very broadly. Careful drawing is none the less essential, however, if their

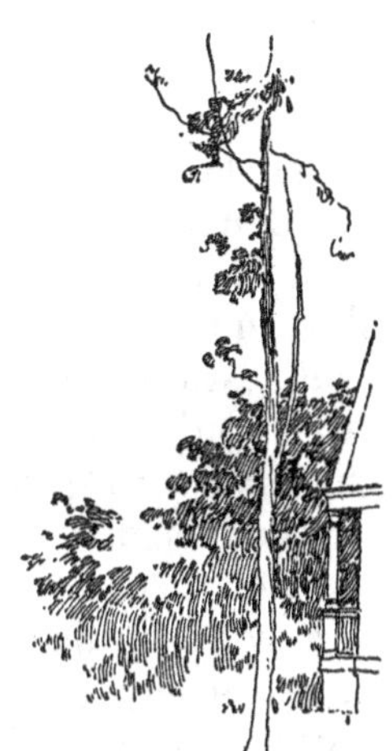

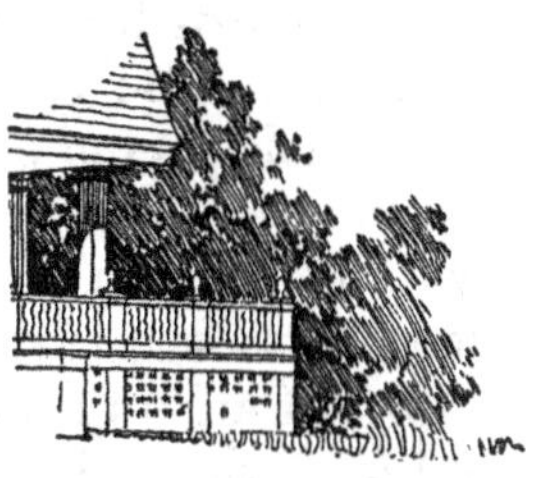

FIG. 47 D. A. GREGG

presence is to be justified; and badly drawn figures furnish a tempting target for the critic of architectural pictures. Certainly, it is only too evident that the people usually seen in such pictures are utterly incapable of taking the slightest interest whatever in architecture, or in anything else; and not infrequently they seem to be even more immovable objects than the buildings themselves, so fixed and inflexible are they. Such figures as these only detract from the interest of the drawing, instead of adding to it, and the draughtsman who has no special aptitude is wise in either omitting them altogether, or in using very few, and is perhaps still wiser if he entrusts the drawing of these to one of his associates more accomplished in this special direction.

The first thing to decide in the matter of figures is their arrangement and grouping, and when this has been determined they should be sketched in lightly in pencil. In this connection a few words by way of suggestion may be found useful. Be careful to avoid anything like an equal spacing of the figures. Group the people interestingly. I have seen as many as thirty individuals in a drawing, no two of whom seemed to be acquainted,—a very unhappy condition of affairs even from a purely pictorial point of view. Do not over-emphasize the base of a building by stringing all the figures along the sidewalks. The lines of the curbs would thus confine and frame them in unpleasantly. Break the continuity of the street lines with figures or carriages in the roadway, as in Fig. 55. After the figures have been satisfactorily arranged, they ought to be carefully drawn as to outline. In doing so, take pains to vary the postures, giving them action, and avoiding the stiff, wooden, fashion-plate type of person so common to architectural drawings. When the time comes to render these accessories with the pen (and this ought, by the way, to be the last thing done) do not lose the freedom and breadth of the drawing by dwelling too long on them. Rise superior to such details as the patterns of neckties.

We will now consider the application to architectural subjects of the remarks on technique and color contained in the previous chapters.

Architectural Textures

To learn to render the different textures of the materials used in architecture, the student would do well to examine and study the methods of prominent illustrators, and then proceed to forget them, developing meanwhile a method of his own. It will be instructive for him, however, as showing the opportunity for play of individuality, to notice how very different, for instance, is Mr. Gregg's manner of rendering brick work to that of Mr. Railton. Compare Figs. 48 and 49. One is splendidly broad,—almost decorative,—the other intimate and picturesque. The work of both these men is eminently worthy of study. For the sophisticated simplicity and directness of his method and the almost severe conscientiousness of his drawing, no less than for his masterly knowledge of black and white, no safer guide could be commended to the young architectural pen-man for the study of principles than Mr. Gregg. Architectural illustration in America owes much to his influence

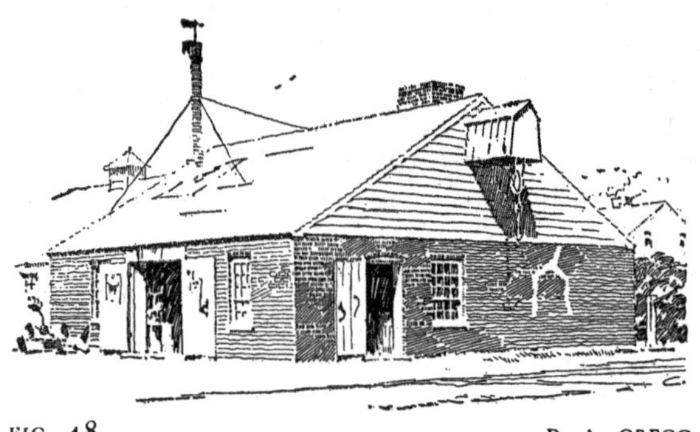

FIG. 48 D. A. GREGG

and, indeed, he may be said to have furnished it with a grammar. Take his drawing of the English cottages, Fig. 50. It is a masterly piece of pen work. There is not a feeble or tentative stroke in the whole of it. The color is brilliant and the textures are expressed with wonderful skill. The student ought to carefully observe the rendering of the various roofs. Notice how the character of the thatch on the second cottage differs from that on the first, and how radically the method of rendering of either varies from that used on the shingle roof at the end of the picture. Compare also the two gable chimneys with each other as well as with the old ruin seen over the tree-tops. Here

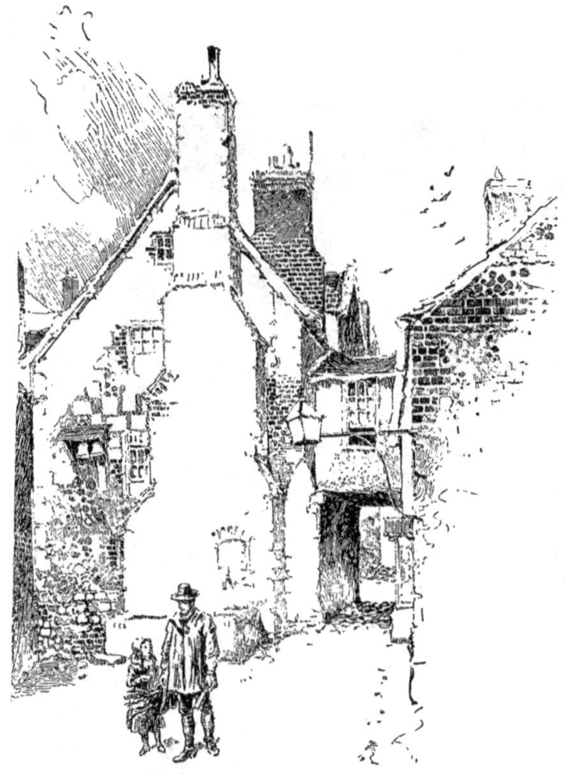

FIG. 49 HERBERT RAILTON

is a drawing by an architectural draughtsman of an architectural *actuality* and not of an artificial abstraction. This is a fairer ground on which to meet the illustrators of the picturesque.

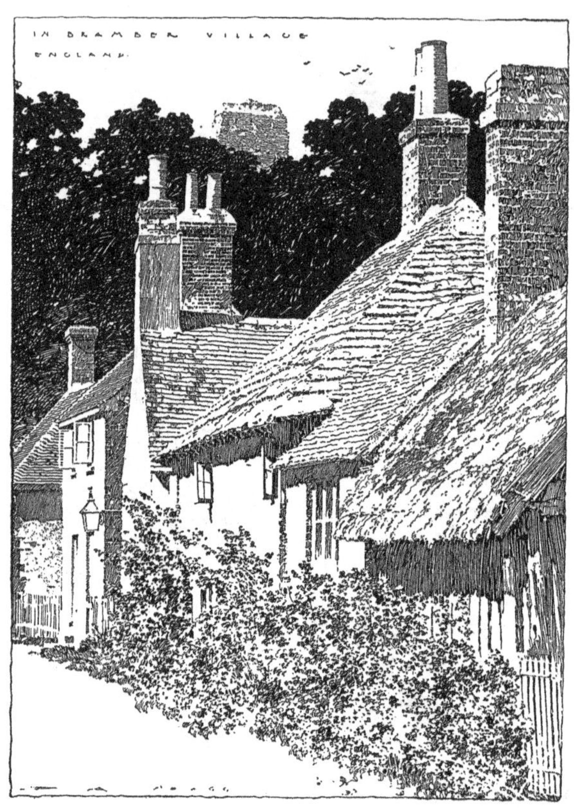

FIG. 50 D. A. GREGG

Examples

Mr. Campbell's drawing, Fig. 51, is a very good example of the rendering of stone textures. The old masonry is capitally expressed by the short irregular line. The student is

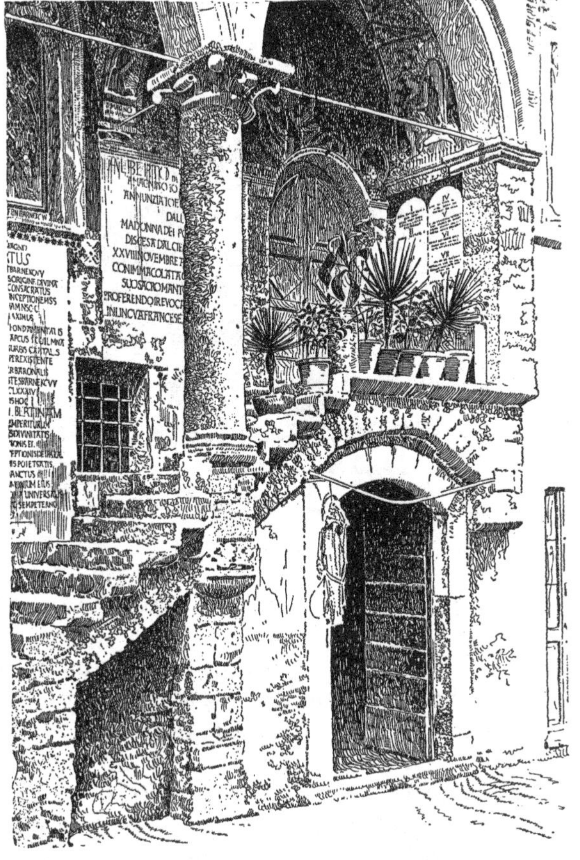

FIG. 51 WALTER M. CAMPBELL

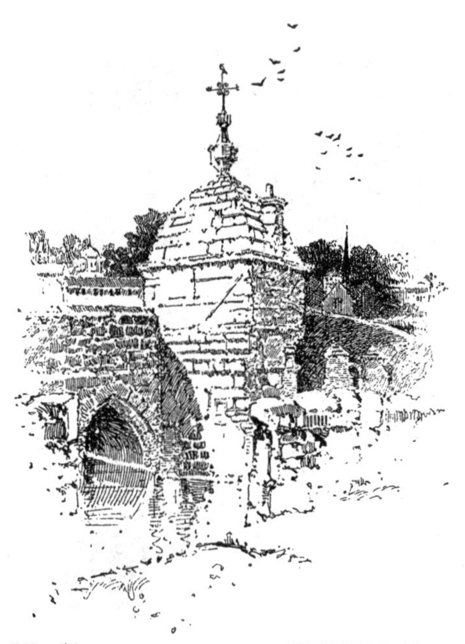

FIG. 52 HERBERT RAILTON

advised to select some portion of this, as well as of the preceding example to copy, using, no matter how small the drawings he may make, a pen not smaller than number 303. I know of no architectural illustrator who hits stonework off quite so cleverly as Mr. Goodhue. Notice, in his drawing of the masonry, in Fig. 8, how the stones are picked out and rendered individually in places and how this intimate treatment is confined to the top of

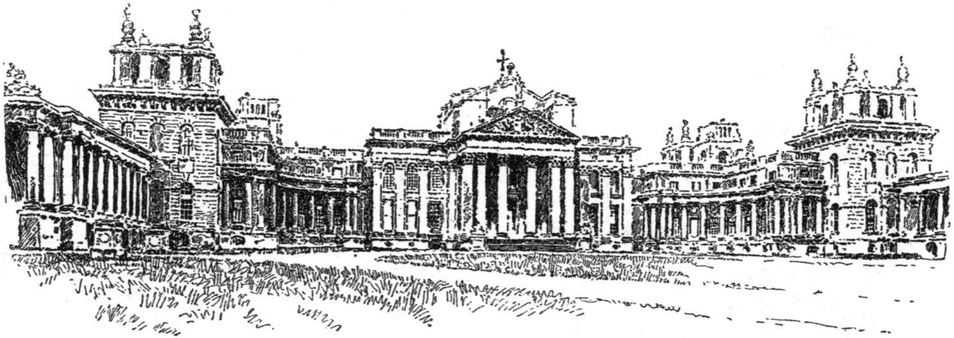

FIG. 53 A. F. JACCACI

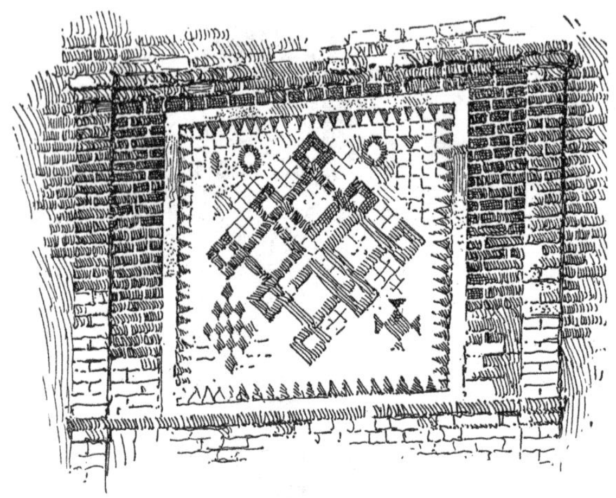

FIG. 54 C. F. BRAGDON

the tower where it tells against the textures of the various roofs and how it is then merged in a broad gray tone which is carried to the street. Mr. Railton's sketches are full of clever suggestion for the architectural illustrator in the way of texture. Figs. 7 and 52 show his free rendering of masonry. The latter is an especially very good subject for study. Observe how well the texture tells in the high portion of the abutment by reason of the thick, broken lines. For a distant effect of stone texture, the drawing by Mr. Jaccaci, Fig. 53, is a fine example. In this the rendering is confined merely to the organic lines of the architecture, and yet the texture is capitally expressed by

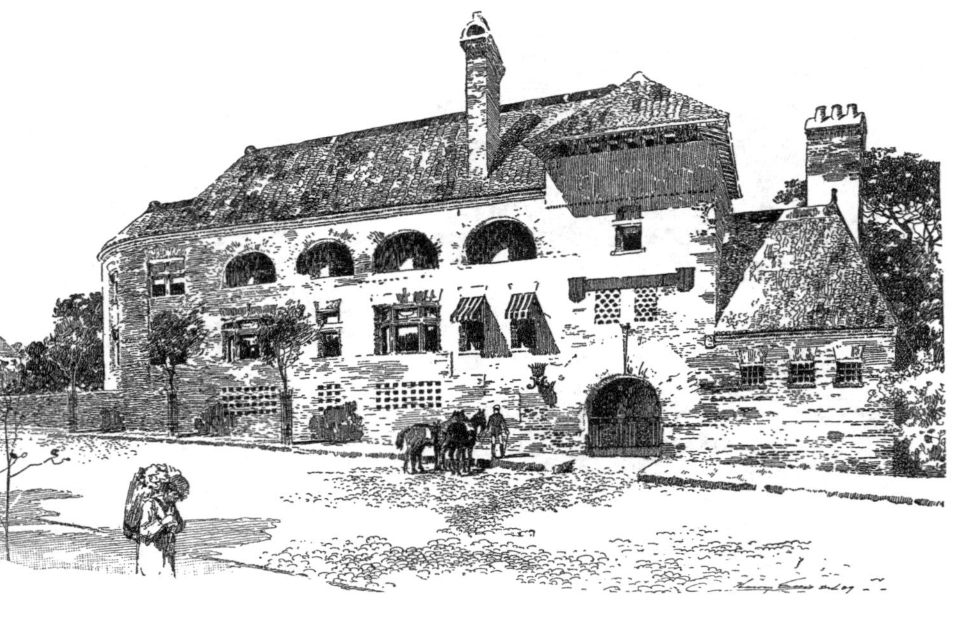

FIG. 55 HARVEY ELLIS

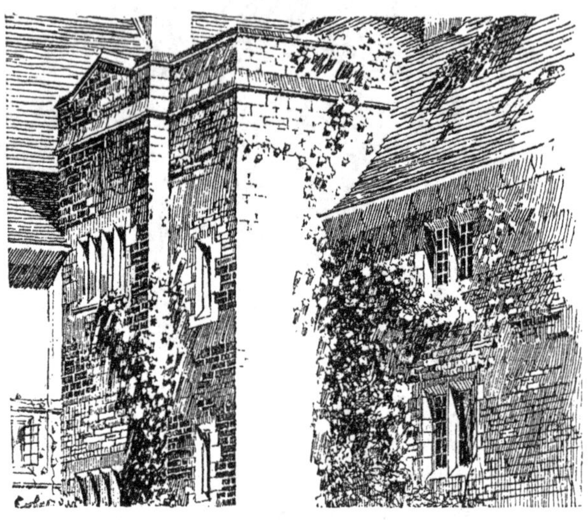

FIG. 56 C. E. MALLOWS

the quality of the stroke, which is loose and much broken. The general result is extremely crisp and pleasing. For broad rendering of brick textures, perhaps there is no one who shows such a masterly method as Mr. Gregg. As may be seen in his sketch of the blacksmith shop, Fig. 48, he employs an irregular dragging line with a great deal of feeling. The brick panel by Mr. Bragdon, Fig. 54, is a neat piece of work. There is excellent texture, too, in the picturesque drawing by Mr. Harvey Ellis, Fig. 55: — observe the rendering of the rough brick surface at the left side of the building. A more intimate treatment is that illustrated in the detail by Mr. C. E. Mallows, the English draughtsman, Fig. 56. In this drawing, however, the edges of the building are unpleasantly hard, and are somewhat out of character with the quaint rendering of the surfaces. Mr. Goodhue uses a similar treatment, and, I think, rather more successfully. On the whole, the broader method, where the texture is carried out more uniformly, is more to be commended, at least for the study of the beginner. Some examples of shingle and slate textures are illustrated by Fig. 57. It is advisable to employ a larger pen for the shingle, so as to ensure the requisite coarseness of effect.

An Architectural Problem

To favorably illustrate an architectural subject it will be found generally expedient to give prominence to one particular elevation in the perspective, the other being permitted to vanish sharply. Fig. 58 may be said to be a fairly typical problem for the architectural penman. The old building on the right, it must be understood, is not a mere accessory, but is an essential part of the picture. The matter of surroundings is the first we have to decide upon, and these ought always to be disposed with reference to the particular form of composition which the subject may suggest. Were we dealing with the foreground building alone there would be no difficulty in adjusting the

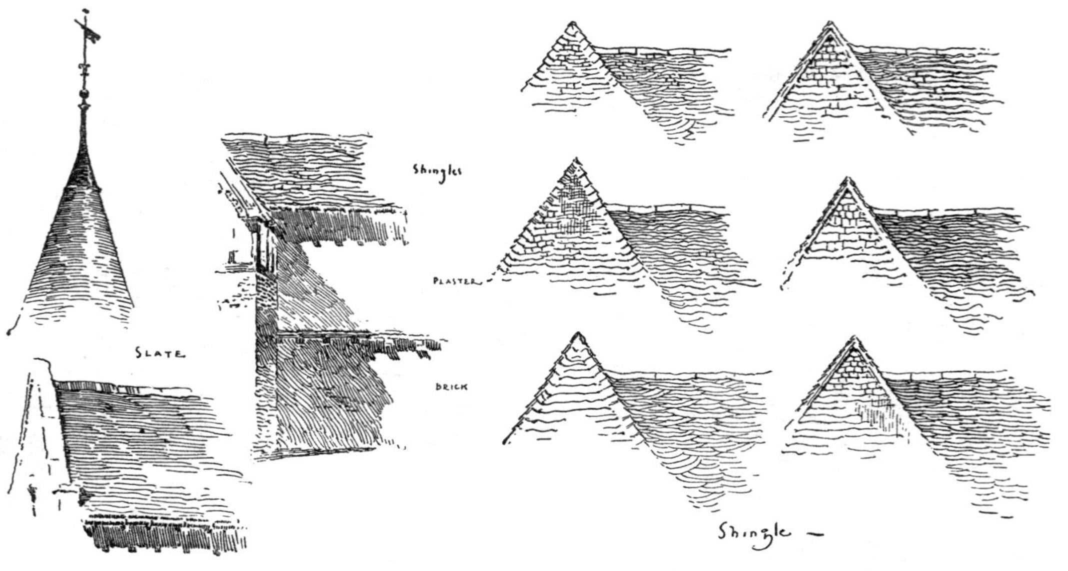

FIG. 57

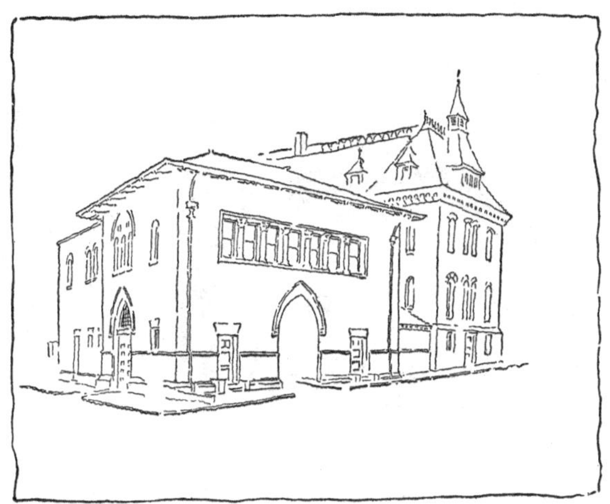

FIG. 58 C. D. M.

oval or the diamond form of composition to it.* As it is, the difficulty lies in the long crested roof-line which takes the same oblique angle as the line of the street, and the influence of this line must be, as far as possible, counteracted. Now the heavy over-hang of the principal roof will naturally cast a shadow which will be an important line in the composition, so we arrange our accessories at the right of the picture in reference to this. Observe that the line of the eaves, if continued, would intersect the top of the gable chimney. The dwelling and the tree then form a focus

*See footnote on page 62.

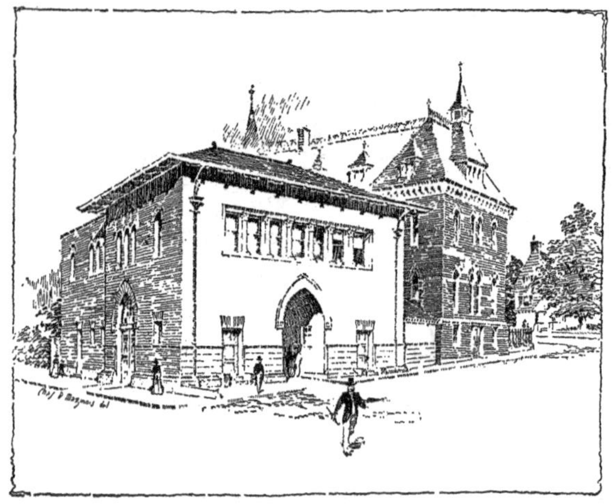

FIG. 59 C. D. M.

for the converging lines of sidewalk and roof, thus qualifying the vertical effect of the building on the right. As the obliquity of the composition is still objectionable, we decide to introduce a foreground figure which will break up the line of the long sidewalk, and place it so that it will increase the influence of some contrary line, see Fig. 59. We find that by putting it a little to the right of the entrance and on a line with that of the left sidewalk, the picture is pleasingly balanced.

We are now ready to consider the disposition of the values. As I have said before, these are determined by the scheme of light and shade. For this reason any given subject may be variously treated. We do not necessarily seek the scheme which will make the most pictorial effect, however, but the one which will serve to set off the building to the best advantage. It is apparent that the most intelligible idea of the form of the structure will be given by shading one side; and, as the front is the more important and the more interesting elevation, on which we need sunlight to give expression to the composition, it is natural to shade the other, thus affording a foil for the bright effects on the front. This bright effect will be further enhanced if we assume that the local color of the roof is darker than that of the walls, so that we can give it a gray tone, which will also make the main building stand away from the other. If, however, we were to likewise assume that the roof of the other building were darker than its walls, we should be obliged to emphasize the objectionable roof line, and as, in any case, we want a dark effect lower down on the walls to give relief to our main building, we will assume that the local color of the older walls is darker than that of the new. The shadow of the main cornice we will make quite strong, emphasis being placed on the nearer corner, which is made almost black. This color is repeated in the windows, which, coming as they do in a group, are some of them more filled in than others, to avoid an effect of monotony. The strong note of the drawing is then given by the foreground figure.

Another scheme for the treatment of this same subject is illustrated by Fig. 60. Here,

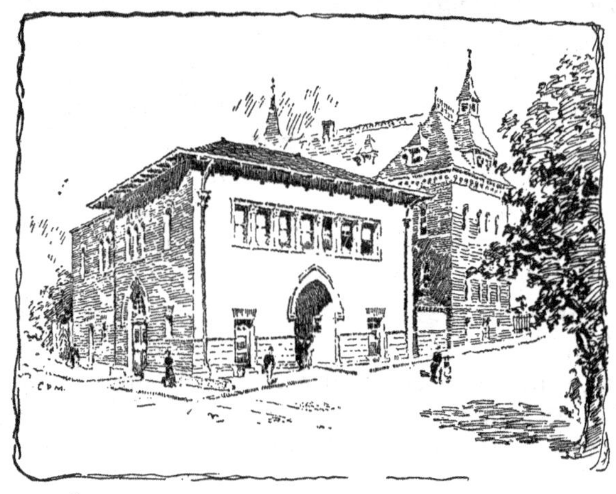

FIG. 60 C. D. M.

by the introduction of the tree at the right of the picture, a triangular composition is adopted. Observe that the sidewalk and roof lines at the left side of the building radiate to the bottom and top of the tree respectively. The shadow of the tree helps to form the bottom line of the triangle. In this case the foreground figure is omitted, as it would have made the triangularity too obvious. In the color-scheme the tree is made the principal dark, and this dark is repeated in the cornice shadow, windows and figures as before. The gray tone of the old building qualifies the blackness of the tree, which would otherwise have made too strong a contrast at the edge of the picture, and so detracted from the interest of the main building.

CHAPTER VII

DECORATIVE DRAWING

In all modern decorative illustration, and, indeed, in all departments of decorative design, the influences of two very different and distinct points of view are noticeable; the one demanding a realistic, the other a purely conventional art. The logic of the first is, that all good pictorial art is essentially decorative; that of the second, that the decorative subject must be designed in organic relation to the space which it is to occupy, and be so treated that the design will primarily fulfil a purely ornamental function. That is to say, whatever of dramatic or literary interest the decorative design may possess must be, as it were, woven into it, so that the general effect shall please as instantly, as directly, and as independently of the meaning, as the pattern of an Oriental rug. The former, it will be seen, is an imitative, the latter an inventive art. In the one, the elements of the subject are rendered with all possible naturalism; while, in the other, effects of atmosphere and the accidental play of light and shade are sacrificed to a conventional rendering, by which the design is kept flat upon the paper or wall. One represents the point of view of the painter and the pictorial illustrator; the other that of the designer and the architect. The second, or conventional idea, has now come to be widely accepted as a true basic principle in decorative art.

The New Decorative School

The idea is not by any means novel; it has always been the fundamental principle of Japanese art; but its genesis was not in Japan. The immediate inspiration of the new Decorative school, as far as it is concerned with the decoration of books, at least, was found in the art of Dürer, Holbein, and the German engravers of the sixteenth century,—interest in which period has been lately so stimulated by the Arts and Crafts movement in England. This movement, which may fairly be regarded as one of the most powerful influences in latter-day art, was begun with the aim of restoring those healthy conditions which obtained before the artist and the craftsman came to be two distinct and very much extranged workers. The activities of the movement were at first more directly concerned with the art of good book-making, which fructified in the famous Kelmscott Press (an institution which, while necessarily undemocratic, has exerted a tremendous influence on modern printing), and to-day there is scarcely any sphere of industrial art which has not been influenced by the Arts and Crafts impetus.

Criticisms of the School

This modern decorative renaissance has a root in sound art principles, which promises for it a vigorous vitality; and perhaps the only serious criticism which has been directed against it is, that it encourages archaic crudities of technique which ignore the high development of the reproductive processes of the present day; and, moreover, that its sympathies tend towards mediæval life and feeling. While such a criticism might reasonably be suggested by the work of some of its individual adherents, it does not touch in the least the essential principles of the school. Art cannot be said to scout modernity because it refuses to adjust itself to the every caprice of Science. The architect rather despises the mechanically perfect brick (very much to the surprise of the manufacturer); and though the camera can record more than the pencil or the brush, yet the artist is not trying to see more than he ever did before. There are, too, many decorative illustrators who, while very distinctly confessing their indebtedness to old examples, are yet perfectly eclectic and individual, both in the choice and development of motive. Take, for example, the very modern subject of the cyclist by Mr. A. B. Frost, Fig. 61. There are no archaisms in it whatever. The drawing is as naturalistic and just as careful as if it were designed for a picture. The shadows, too, are cast, giving an effect of strong

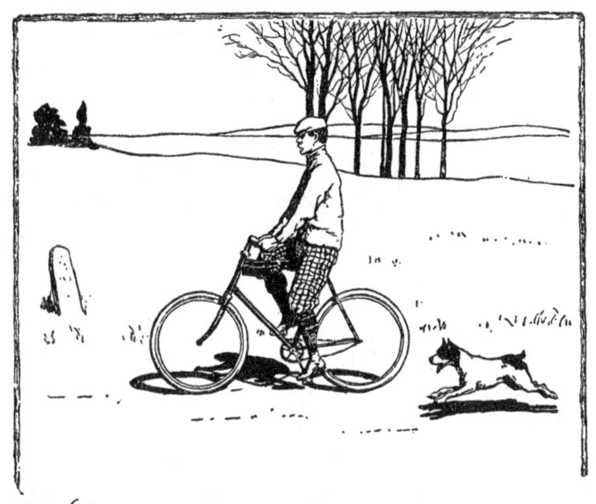

FIG. 61 A. B. FROST

outdoor light; but the treatment, broad and beautifully simple so as to be reconcilable with the lettering which accompanied it, is well within conventional lines. That the character of the technical treatment is such as to place no tax on the mechanical inventiveness of the processman is not inexcusable archæology.

A valuable attribute of this conventional art is, that it puts no bounds to the fancy of the designer. It is a figurative language in which he may get away from commonplace statement. What has always seemed to me a very logical employment of convention appears in the *Punch* cartoons of Sir John Tenniel and Mr. Lindley Sambourne. Even in those cartoons which are devoid of physical caricature (and they are generally free from this), we see at a glance that it is the political and not the personal relations of the personæ that are represented; whereas in the naturalistic cartoons of *Puck*, for example, one cannot resist the feeling that personalities are being roughly handled.

Relation A chief principle in all decorative design and treatment is that of Relation. If the space to be ornamented be a book-page the design and treatment must be such as to harmonize with the printing. The type must be considered as an element in the design, and, as the effect of a page of type is broad and uniformly flat, the ornament must be made to count as broad and flat likewise. The same principle holds equally in mural decoration. There the design ought to be subordinate to the general effect of the architecture. The wall is not to be considered merely as a convenient place on which to plaster a picture, its structural purpose must be regarded, and this cannot be expressed if the design or treatment be purely pictorial — if vague perspective distances and strong foreground accents be used without symmetry or order, except that order which governs itself alone. In other words, the decoration must be organic.

Decorative illustrations may be broadly classified under three heads as follows: First,

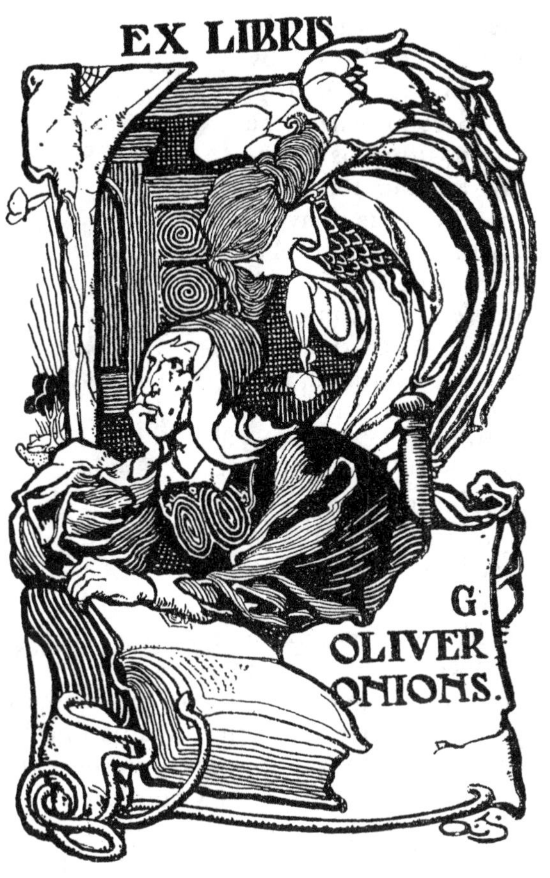

FIG. 62 ALFRED G. JONES

Classes of Decorative Design

those wherein the composition and the treatment are both conventional, as, for example, in the ex-libris by Mr. A. G. Jones, Fig. 62. Second, where the composition is naturalistic, and the treatment only is conventional, as in Mr. Frost's design. Third, where the composition is decorative but not conventional, and the treatment is seminatural, as in the drawing by Mr. Walter Appleton Clark, Fig. 63. (The latter subject is of such a character as to lend itself without convention to a decorative effect; and, although the figure is modeled as in a pictorial illustration, the organic lines are so emphasized throughout as to preserve the decorative character, and the whole keeps its place on the page.) Under this third head would be included those subjects of a pictorial nature whose composition and values are such as to make them reconcilable to a decorative use by means of borders or very defined edges, as in

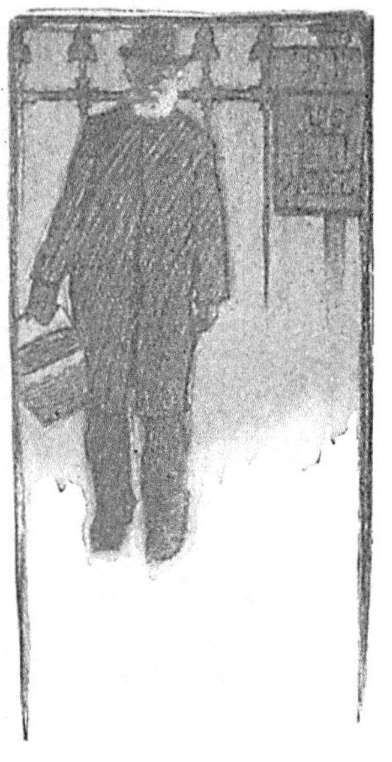

FIG. 63 W. APPLETON CLARK

the illustration by Mr. A. Campbell Cross, Fig. 64.

The Decorative Outline

Another essential characteristic of decorative drawing is the emphasized Outline. This may be heavy or delicate, according to the nature of the subject or individual taste. The designs by Mr. W. Nicholson and Mr. Selwyn Image, for instance, are drawn with a fatness of outline not to be obtained with anything but a brush; while the outlines of M. Boutet de Monvel, marked as they are, are evidently the work of a more than usually fine pen. In each case, however, everything is in keeping with the scale of the outline adopted, so that this always retains its proper emphasis. The decorative outline should never be broken, but should be kept firm, positive, and uniform. It may be

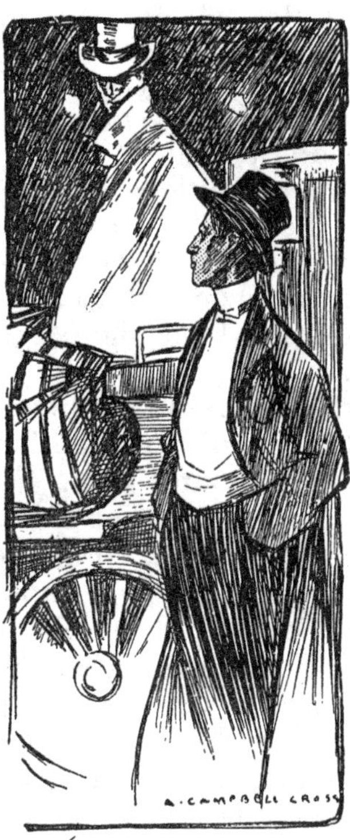

FIG. 64 A. CAMPBELL CROSS

heavy, and yet be rich and feeling, as may be seen in the Mucha design, Fig. 65. Generally speaking, the line ought not to be made with a nervous stroke, but rather with a slow, deliberate drag. The natural wavering of the hand need occasion no anxiety, and, indeed, it is often more helpful to the line than otherwise.

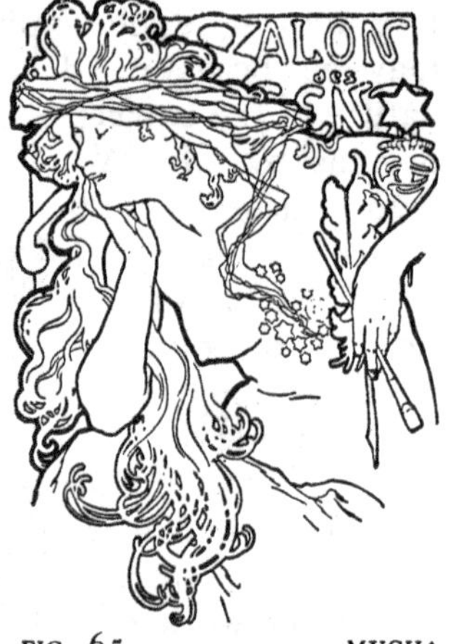

FIG. 65 MUCHA

Perhaps there is no more difficult thing to do well than to model the figure while still preserving the decorative outline. Several examples of the skilful accomplishment of this problem are illustrated here. Observe, for instance, how in the quaint Dürer-like design by Mr. Howard Pyle, Fig. 66, the edges of the drapery-folds are emphasized in the shadow by keeping them white, and see how wonderfully effective the result is. The same device is also to be noticed in the book-plate design by Mr. A. G. Jones, Fig. 62, as well as in the more conventional treatment of the black figure in the Bradley poster, Fig. 67.

In the rendering of decorative subjects, the

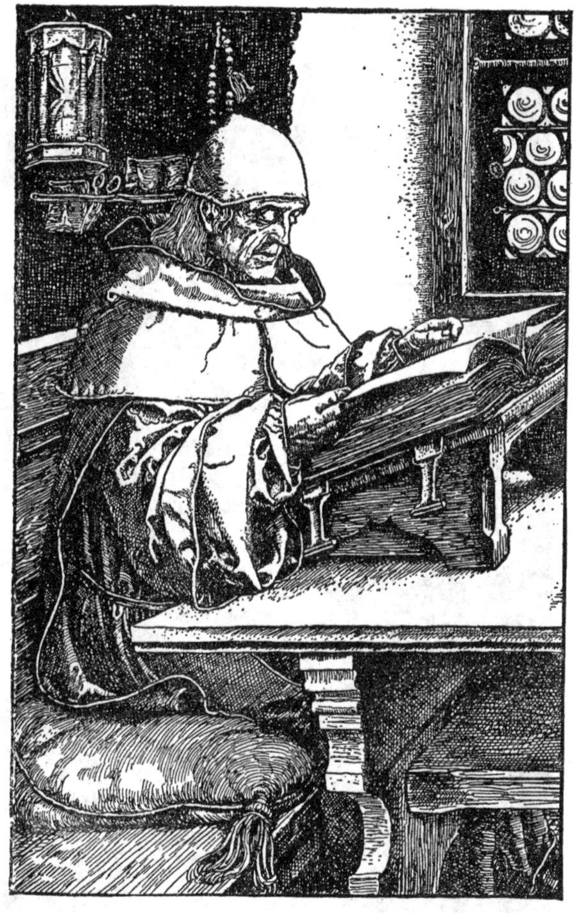

FIG. 66 HOWARD PYLE

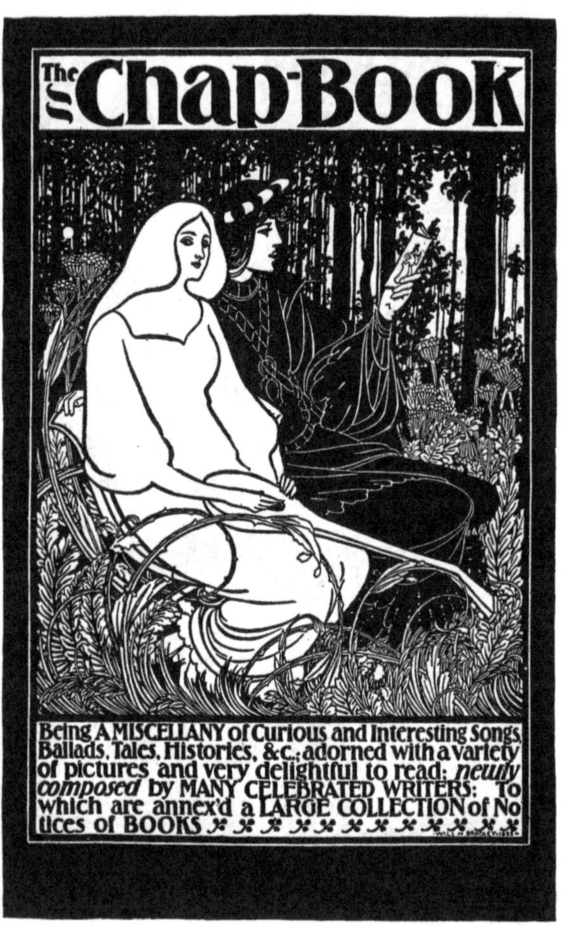

FIG. 67 WILL H. BRADLEY

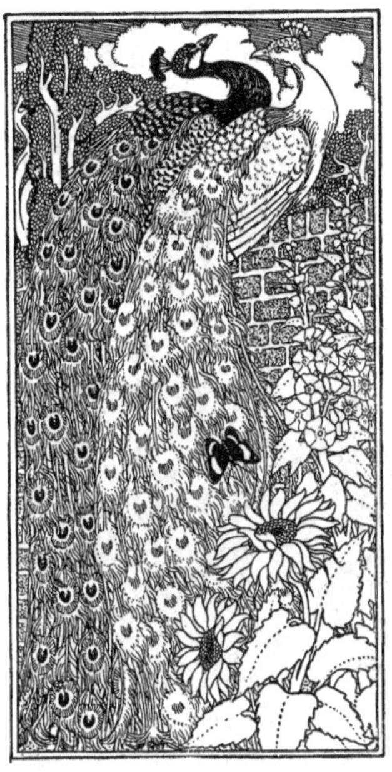

FIG. 68 P. J. BILLINGHURST

Color should be, as much as possible, designed. Whereas a poster, which is made with a view to its entire effect being grasped at once, may be rendered in flat masses of color, the head- or tail-piece for a decorative book-page should be worked out in more detail, and the design should be finer and more varied in color. The more the color is attained by means of pattern, instead of by mere irresponsible lines, the more decorative is the result. Observe the color-making by pattern in the book-plate by Mr. P. J. Billinghurst, Fig. 68. A great variety of textures may be obtained by means of varied patterns without affecting the breadth of the color-scheme. This may be noticed in the design last mentioned, in which the textures are extremely well rendered, as well as in the poster design by Mr. Bradley for the *Chap-Book*, just referred to. *Color*

The color-scheme ought to be simple and broad. No set rules can be laid down to govern its disposition, which must always have reference to the whole design. The importance of employing such a broad and simple scheme in decorative drawing needs no better argument than the effective poster design by the "Beggarstaff Brothers," Fig. 69, and that by Mr. Penfield, Fig. 70. Of course the more conventional the design the less regard need be paid to anything like a logical disposition of color. A figure may be set against a black landscape with white trees without fear of criticism from reasonable people, provided it looks effective there.

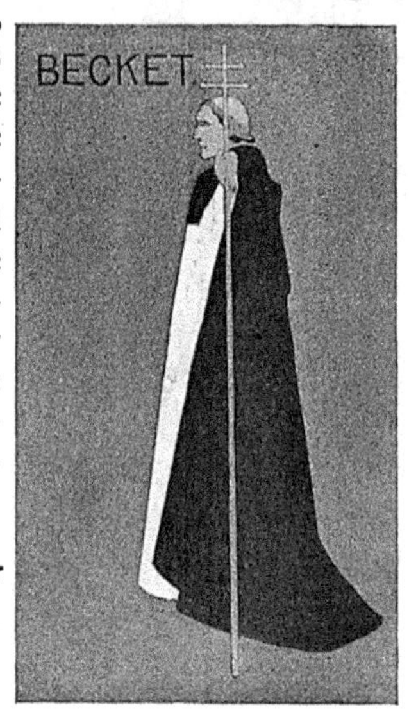

FIG. 69 "BEGGARSTAFF BROTHERS"

Modern Decorative Draughtsmen

A word or two, in conclusion, concerning some of the modern decorative draughtsmen. Of those who work in the sixteenth century manner, Mr. Howard Pyle is unquestionably the superior technician. His line, masterly in its sureness, is rich and charged with feel-

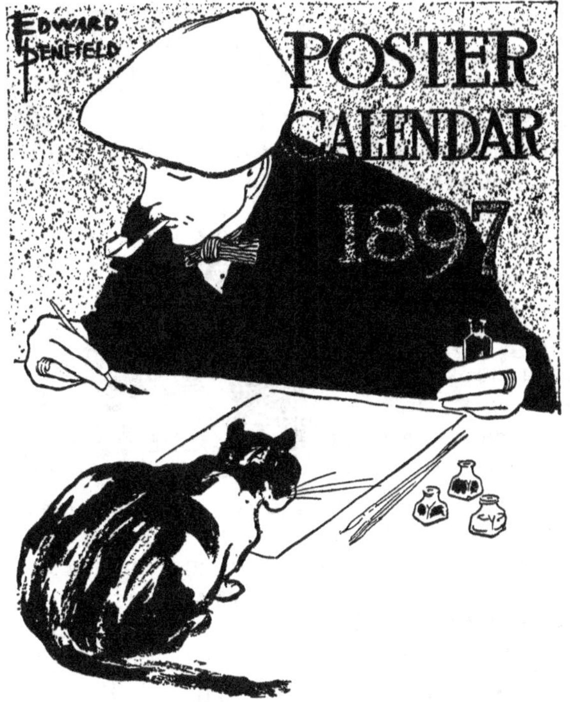

FIG. 70 EDWARD PENFIELD

ing. Mr. H. Ospovat, one of the younger group of English decorators, has also a charming technique, rather freer than that of Mr. Pyle, and yet reminding one of it. Mr. Louis Rhead is another of the same school, whose designs are deserving of study. The example of his work shown in Fig. 71 — excellent both in color and in drawing — is one of his earlier designs. Mr. J. W. Simpson, in the book-plate, Fig. 72, shows the broadest possible decorative method; a method which, while too broad for anything but a poster or a book-label, is just what the student should aim at being able to attain.

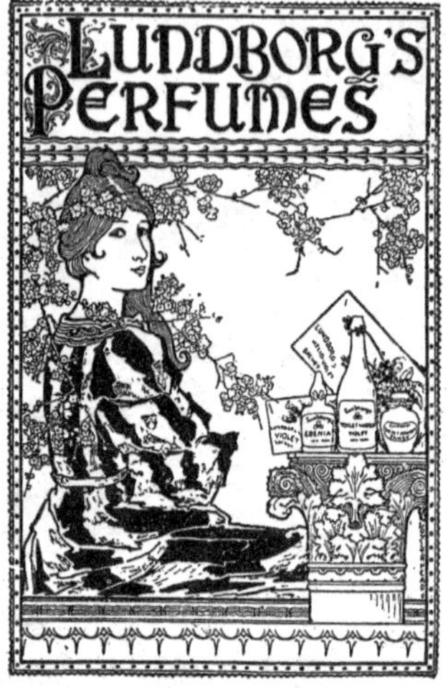

FIG. 71 LOUIS J. RHEAD

Some of those decorators whose work shows a Japanese influence have a most exquisite method. Of these, that remarkable draughtsman, M. Boutet de Monvel, easily takes the first place. Those who have had the good fortune to see his original drawings will not easily forget the delicate beauty of outline nor the won-

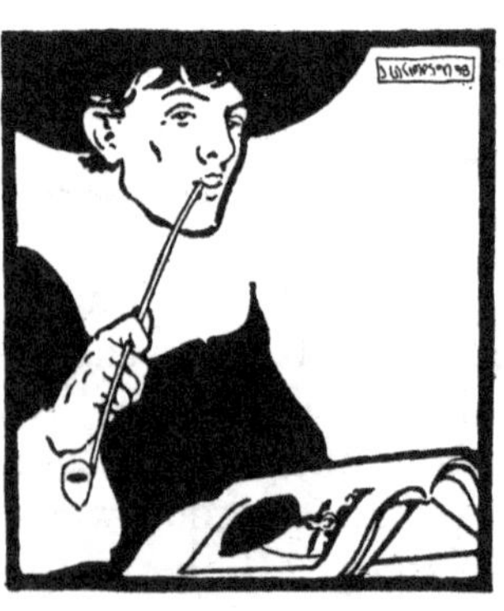

FIG. 72 J. W. SIMPSON

derfully tender coloring which distinguishes them. Mr. Maxfield Parrish is another masterly decorator who is noted for his free use of Japanese precedent as well as for the resourcefulness of his technique. The drawings of Mr. Henry McCarter, too, executed as they are in pure line, are especially valuable to the student of the pen. In respect both of the design and treatment of decorative subjects, the work of the late Aubrey Beardsley is more individual than that of any other modern draughtsman. That of our own clever and eccentric Bradley, while very clearly confessing its obligations, has yet a distinctive character of its own. The work of the two latter draughtsmen, however, is not to be recommended to the unsophisticated beginner for imitation, for it is likely to be more harmful than otherwise. Nevertheless, by steering clear of the grotesque conventions with which they treat the human figure, by carefully avoiding the intense blacks in which a great deal of their work abounds, and by generally maintaining a healthy condition of mind, much is to be learned from a study of their peculiar methods.

A CATALOG OF SELECTED

DOVER BOOKS

IN ALL FIELDS OF INTEREST

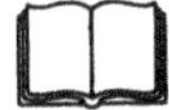

A CATALOG OF SELECTED DOVER BOOKS IN ALL FIELDS OF INTEREST

100 BEST-LOVED POEMS, Edited by Philip Smith. "The Passionate Shepherd to His Love," "Shall I compare thee to a summer's day?" "Death, be not proud," "The Raven," "The Road Not Taken," plus works by Blake, Wordsworth, Byron, Shelley, Keats, many others. 96pp. 5$\frac{3}{16}$ x 8$\frac{1}{4}$. 0-486-28553-7

100 SMALL HOUSES OF THE THIRTIES, Brown-Blodgett Company. Exterior photographs and floor plans for 100 charming structures. Illustrations of models accompanied by descriptions of interiors, color schemes, closet space, and other amenities. 200 illustrations. 112pp. 8$\frac{3}{8}$ x 11. 0-486-44131-8

1000 TURN-OF-THE-CENTURY HOUSES: With Illustrations and Floor Plans, Herbert C. Chivers. Reproduced from a rare edition, this showcase of homes ranges from cottages and bungalows to sprawling mansions. Each house is meticulously illustrated and accompanied by complete floor plans. 256pp. 9$\frac{3}{8}$ x 12$\frac{1}{4}$. 0-486-45596-3

101 GREAT AMERICAN POEMS, Edited by The American Poetry & Literacy Project. Rich treasury of verse from the 19th and 20th centuries includes works by Edgar Allan Poe, Robert Frost, Walt Whitman, Langston Hughes, Emily Dickinson, T. S. Eliot, other notables. 96pp. 5$\frac{3}{16}$ x 8$\frac{1}{4}$. 0-486-40158-8

101 GREAT SAMURAI PRINTS, Utagawa Kuniyoshi. Kuniyoshi was a master of the warrior woodblock print — and these 18th-century illustrations represent the pinnacle of his craft. Full-color portraits of renowned Japanese samurais pulse with movement, passion, and remarkably fine detail. 112pp. 8$\frac{3}{8}$ x 11. 0-486-46523-3

ABC OF BALLET, Janet Grosser. Clearly worded, abundantly illustrated little guide defines basic ballet-related terms: arabesque, battement, pas de chat, relevé, sissonne, many others. Pronunciation guide included. Excellent primer. 48pp. 4$\frac{3}{16}$ x 5$\frac{3}{4}$. 0-486-40871-X

ACCESSORIES OF DRESS: An Illustrated Encyclopedia, Katherine Lester and Bess Viola Oerke. Illustrations of hats, veils, wigs, cravats, shawls, shoes, gloves, and other accessories enhance an engaging commentary that reveals the humor and charm of the many-sided story of accessorized apparel. 644 figures and 59 plates. 608pp. 6 $\frac{1}{8}$ x 9$\frac{1}{4}$. 0-486-43378-1

ADVENTURES OF HUCKLEBERRY FINN, Mark Twain. Join Huck and Jim as their boyhood adventures along the Mississippi River lead them into a world of excitement, danger, and self-discovery. Humorous narrative, lyrical descriptions of the Mississippi valley, and memorable characters. 224pp. 5$\frac{3}{16}$ x 8$\frac{1}{4}$. 0-486-28061-6

ALICE STARMORE'S BOOK OF FAIR ISLE KNITTING, Alice Starmore. A noted designer from the region of Scotland's Fair Isle explores the history and techniques of this distinctive, stranded-color knitting style and provides copious illustrated instructions for 14 original knitwear designs. 208pp. 8$\frac{3}{8}$ x 10$\frac{7}{8}$. 0-486-47218-3

Browse over 9,000 books at www.doverpublications.com

THE BATTLES THAT CHANGED HISTORY, Fletcher Pratt. Historian profiles 16 crucial conflicts, ancient to modern, that changed the course of Western civilization. Gripping accounts of battles led by Alexander the Great, Joan of Arc, Ulysses S. Grant, other commanders. 27 maps. 352pp. 5⅜ x 8½. 0-486-41129-X

BEETHOVEN'S LETTERS, Ludwig van Beethoven. Edited by Dr. A. C. Kalischer. Features 457 letters to fellow musicians, friends, greats, patrons, and literary men. Reveals musical thoughts, quirks of personality, insights, and daily events. Includes 15 plates. 410pp. 5⅜ x 8½. 0-486-22769-3

BERNICE BOBS HER HAIR AND OTHER STORIES, F. Scott Fitzgerald. This brilliant anthology includes 6 of Fitzgerald's most popular stories: "The Diamond as Big as the Ritz," the title tale, "The Offshore Pirate," "The Ice Palace," "The Jelly Bean," and "May Day." 176pp. 5⅜ x 8½. 0-486-47049-0

BESLER'S BOOK OF FLOWERS AND PLANTS: 73 Full-Color Plates from Hortus Eystettensis, 1613, Basilius Besler. Here is a selection of magnificent plates from the *Hortus Eystettensis,* which vividly illustrated and identified the plants, flowers, and trees that thrived in the legendary German garden at Eichstätt. 80pp. 8⅜ x 11. 0-486-46005-3

THE BOOK OF KELLS, Edited by Blanche Cirker. Painstakingly reproduced from a rare facsimile edition, this volume contains full-page decorations, portraits, illustrations, plus a sampling of textual leaves with exquisite calligraphy and ornamentation. 32 full-color illustrations. 32pp. 9⅜ x 12¼. 0-486-24345-1

THE BOOK OF THE CROSSBOW: With an Additional Section on Catapults and Other Siege Engines, Ralph Payne-Gallwey. Fascinating study traces history and use of crossbow as military and sporting weapon, from Middle Ages to modern times. Also covers related weapons: balistas, catapults, Turkish bows, more. Over 240 illustrations. 400pp. 7¼ x 10⅝. 0-486-28720-3

THE BUNGALOW BOOK: Floor Plans and Photos of 112 Houses, 1910, Henry L. Wilson. Here are 112 of the most popular and economic blueprints of the early 20th century — plus an illustration or photograph of each completed house. A wonderful time capsule that still offers a wealth of valuable insights. 160pp. 8⅜ x 11. 0-486-45104-6

THE CALL OF THE WILD, Jack London. A classic novel of adventure, drawn from London's own experiences as a Klondike adventurer, relating the story of a heroic dog caught in the brutal life of the Alaska Gold Rush. Note. 64pp. 5$\frac{3}{16}$ x 8¼. 0-486-26472-6

CANDIDE, Voltaire. Edited by Francois-Marie Arouet. One of the world's great satires since its first publication in 1759. Witty, caustic skewering of romance, science, philosophy, religion, government — nearly all human ideals and institutions. 112pp. 5$\frac{3}{16}$ x 8¼. 0-486-26689-3

CELEBRATED IN THEIR TIME: Photographic Portraits from the George Grantham Bain Collection, Edited by Amy Pastan. With an Introduction by Michael Carlebach. Remarkable portrait gallery features 112 rare images of Albert Einstein, Charlie Chaplin, the Wright Brothers, Henry Ford, and other luminaries from the worlds of politics, art, entertainment, and industry. 128pp. 8⅜ x 11. 0-486-46754-6

CHARIOTS FOR APOLLO: The NASA History of Manned Lunar Spacecraft to 1969, Courtney G. Brooks, James M. Grimwood, and Loyd S. Swenson, Jr. This illustrated history by a trio of experts is the definitive reference on the Apollo spacecraft and lunar modules. It traces the vehicles' design, development, and operation in space. More than 100 photographs and illustrations. 576pp. 6¾ x 9¼. 0-486-46756-2

A CHRISTMAS CAROL, Charles Dickens. This engrossing tale relates Ebenezer Scrooge's ghostly journeys through Christmases past, present, and future and his ultimate transformation from a harsh and grasping old miser to a charitable and compassionate human being. 80pp. 5$\frac{3}{16}$ x 8$\frac{1}{4}$. 0-486-26865-9

COMMON SENSE, Thomas Paine. First published in January of 1776, this highly influential landmark document clearly and persuasively argued for American separation from Great Britain and paved the way for the Declaration of Independence. 64pp. 5$\frac{3}{16}$ x 8$\frac{1}{4}$. 0-486-29602-4

THE COMPLETE SHORT STORIES OF OSCAR WILDE, Oscar Wilde. Complete texts of "The Happy Prince and Other Tales," "A House of Pomegranates," "Lord Arthur Savile's Crime and Other Stories," "Poems in Prose," and "The Portrait of Mr. W. H." 208pp. 5$\frac{3}{16}$ x 8$\frac{1}{4}$. 0-486-45216-6

COMPLETE SONNETS, William Shakespeare. Over 150 exquisite poems deal with love, friendship, the tyranny of time, beauty's evanescence, death, and other themes in language of remarkable power, precision, and beauty. Glossary of archaic terms. 80pp. 5$\frac{3}{16}$ x 8$\frac{1}{4}$. 0-486-26686-9

THE COUNT OF MONTE CRISTO: Abridged Edition, Alexandre Dumas. Falsely accused of treason, Edmond Dantès is imprisoned in the bleak Chateau d'If. After a hair-raising escape, he launches an elaborate plot to extract a bitter revenge against those who betrayed him. 448pp. 5$\frac{3}{16}$ x 8$\frac{1}{4}$. 0-486-45643-9

CRAFTSMAN BUNGALOWS: Designs from the Pacific Northwest, Yoho & Merritt. This reprint of a rare catalog, showcasing the charming simplicity and cozy style of Craftsman bungalows, is filled with photos of completed homes, plus floor plans and estimated costs. An indispensable resource for architects, historians, and illustrators. 112pp. 10 x 7. 0-486-46875-5

CRAFTSMAN BUNGALOWS: 59 Homes from "The Craftsman," Edited by Gustav Stickley. Best and most attractive designs from Arts and Crafts Movement publication — 1903–1916 — includes sketches, photographs of homes, floor plans, descriptive text. 128pp. 8$\frac{1}{4}$ x 11. 0-486-25829-7

CRIME AND PUNISHMENT, Fyodor Dostoyevsky. Translated by Constance Garnett. Supreme masterpiece tells the story of Raskolnikov, a student tormented by his own thoughts after he murders an old woman. Overwhelmed by guilt and terror, he confesses and goes to prison. 480pp. 5$\frac{3}{16}$ x 8$\frac{1}{4}$. 0-486-41587-2

THE DECLARATION OF INDEPENDENCE AND OTHER GREAT DOCUMENTS OF AMERICAN HISTORY: 1775-1865, Edited by John Grafton. Thirteen compelling and influential documents: Henry's "Give Me Liberty or Give Me Death," Declaration of Independence, The Constitution, Washington's First Inaugural Address, The Monroe Doctrine, The Emancipation Proclamation, Gettysburg Address, more. 64pp. 5$\frac{3}{16}$ x 8$\frac{1}{4}$. 0-486-41124-9

THE DESERT AND THE SOWN: Travels in Palestine and Syria, Gertrude Bell. "The female Lawrence of Arabia," Gertrude Bell wrote captivating, perceptive accounts of her travels in the Middle East. This intriguing narrative, accompanied by 160 photos, traces her 1905 sojourn in Lebanon, Syria, and Palestine. 368pp. 5$\frac{3}{8}$ x 8$\frac{1}{2}$. 0-486-46876-3

A DOLL'S HOUSE, Henrik Ibsen. Ibsen's best-known play displays his genius for realistic prose drama. An expression of women's rights, the play climaxes when the central character, Nora, rejects a smothering marriage and life in "a doll's house." 80pp. 5$\frac{3}{16}$ x 8$\frac{1}{4}$. 0-486-27062-9

DOOMED SHIPS: Great Ocean Liner Disasters, William H. Miller, Jr. Nearly 200 photographs, many from private collections, highlight tales of some of the vessels whose pleasure cruises ended in catastrophe: the *Morro Castle, Normandie, Andrea Doria, Europa,* and many others. 128pp. 8⅞ x 11¾. 0-486-45366-9

THE DORÉ BIBLE ILLUSTRATIONS, Gustave Doré. Detailed plates from the Bible: the Creation scenes, Adam and Eve, horrifying visions of the Flood, the battle sequences with their monumental crowds, depictions of the life of Jesus, 241 plates in all. 241pp. 9 x 12. 0-486-23004-X

DRAWING DRAPERY FROM HEAD TO TOE, Cliff Young. Expert guidance on how to draw shirts, pants, skirts, gloves, hats, and coats on the human figure, including folds in relation to the body, pull and crush, action folds, creases, more. Over 200 drawings. 48pp. 8¼ x 11. 0-486-45591-2

DUBLINERS, James Joyce. A fine and accessible introduction to the work of one of the 20th century's most influential writers, this collection features 15 tales, including a masterpiece of the short-story genre, "The Dead." 160pp. 5$\frac{3}{16}$ x 8¼. 0-486-26870-5

EASY-TO-MAKE POP-UPS, Joan Irvine. Illustrated by Barbara Reid. Dozens of wonderful ideas for three-dimensional paper fun — from holiday greeting cards with moving parts to a pop-up menagerie. Easy-to-follow, illustrated instructions for more than 30 projects. 299 black-and-white illustrations. 96pp. 8⅜ x 11. 0-486-44622-0

EASY-TO-MAKE STORYBOOK DOLLS: A "Novel" Approach to Cloth Dollmaking, Sherralyn St. Clair. Favorite fictional characters come alive in this unique beginner's dollmaking guide. Includes patterns for Pollyanna, Dorothy from *The Wonderful Wizard of Oz,* Mary of *The Secret Garden,* plus easy-to-follow instructions, 263 black-and-white illustrations, and an 8-page color insert. 112pp. 8¼ x 11. 0-486-47360-0

EINSTEIN'S ESSAYS IN SCIENCE, Albert Einstein. Speeches and essays in accessible, everyday language profile influential physicists such as Niels Bohr and Isaac Newton. They also explore areas of physics to which the author made major contributions. 128pp. 5 x 8. 0-486-47011-3

EL DORADO: Further Adventures of the Scarlet Pimpernel, Baroness Orczy. A popular sequel to *The Scarlet Pimpernel,* this suspenseful story recounts the Pimpernel's attempts to rescue the Dauphin from imprisonment during the French Revolution. An irresistible blend of intrigue, period detail, and vibrant characterizations. 352pp. 5$\frac{3}{16}$ x 8¼. 0-486-44026-5

ELEGANT SMALL HOMES OF THE TWENTIES: 99 Designs from a Competition, Chicago Tribune. Nearly 100 designs for five- and six-room houses feature New England and Southern colonials, Normandy cottages, stately Italianate dwellings, and other fascinating snapshots of American domestic architecture of the 1920s. 112pp. 9 x 12. 0-486-46910-7

THE ELEMENTS OF STYLE: The Original Edition, William Strunk, Jr. This is the book that generations of writers have relied upon for timeless advice on grammar, diction, syntax, and other essentials. In concise terms, it identifies the principal requirements of proper style and common errors. 64pp. 5⅜ x 8½. 0-486-44798-7

THE ELUSIVE PIMPERNEL, Baroness Orczy. Robespierre's revolutionaries find their wicked schemes thwarted by the heroic Pimpernel — Sir Percival Blakeney. In this thrilling sequel, Chauvelin devises a plot to eliminate the Pimpernel and his wife. 272pp. 5$\frac{3}{16}$ x 8¼. 0-486-45464-9